CREATE STORY CONFLICT

HOW TO INCREASE TENSION IN YOUR WRITING & KEEP READERS TURNING PAGES

EILEEN COOK

CREATIVE ACADEMY FOR WRITERS

CONTENTS

To my partners in business and crime - Crystal, Donna and Stephanie. Here's to not having any conflict with us.

A note about spelling...

The three founding members of The Creative Academy for Writers live in Canada, and we made a conscious decision to use Canadian spellings throughout our book series. Because...well...it's who we are, eh?!

A note to our American readers and other friends from around the world... we welcome U in Canada :) Thanks for your willingness to learn new things and play nice with your colourful Canadian neighbours!

While we always appreciate readers letting us know if you find errors in our books, pretty please double check Canadian spellings before you tell us we're wrong!

When we're quoting someone and the quote had American spellings, we left those intact.

xo Eileen, Crystal and Donna

THE PHILOSOPHY OF THE CREATIVE ACADEMY

Like most writers, I started as a reader. I would go to the library every week with my parents to check out a huge stack of books. When I realized that someone was responsible for making up those stories, I knew that was what I wanted to do. I got in the habit of running my finger down the shelves to the place where my (as yet completely unwritten) book would go. Then I'd jam my hand in there and shove the books on either side over a bit to make room for me. One day there was already a space made. The children's librarian came over and whispered, "Don't worry, I'm saving room for you."

She was one of the first people to believe in my dream of being a writer.

We writers need someone to believe in our dream and hold us up when we feel like letting go. Choosing to write takes courage. Courage to continue to try when the words won't come. Courage to share your work with others and invite their feedback. Courage to send it off into the world, through agents and editors or by indie publishing your story. The bad news is that the world has too many people who will tell you your dream is foolish and, instead of encouraging you, will go out of their way to *discourage* you. It's easier for them to tear down someone else's dream than to work toward one of their own. So you need to surround yourself with the right people.

That's why we started The Creative Academy for Writers. We wanted to create a place that fostered big dreams for writers and at the same time provided practical guidance to reach them. We wanted to build a community of like-minded people, offer encouragement and practical support, and assist people in taking the next steps on their writing journey. We wanted to be that voice in your ear that says "you got this" when you feel like you very much don't.

This book is a part of that journey for you. If you aren't already a member, we hope you'll consider joining us online at The Creative Academy for Writers. It's free (yes, you read that right) and a community is always stronger when it grows to include great people. And don't worry— we're making some space on the shelves for you. There's always room.

HOW TO GET THE MOST FROM
THIS BOOK

Conflict is tricky. Most of us don't like it and tend to avoid it. Others love it and fire up their rage machine at every opportunity. (It is possible social media was created simply to give those people somewhere to hang out.) This book is designed to help you understand conflict and ramp it up on the page because like it or not, conflict is vital for a novel.

In this book I'll talk about why conflict is so important, explain different kinds of conflict, and give you some practical ways to increase it in your book. It's up to you to decide how conflict will impact your story, and you'll see that I'm not someone who believes there is only one right way to do anything. Please take and use what is most helpful for you in this process. If you join us in the Creative Academy you'll see I've been talking about conflict for a long time. There is a masterclass and may office hours recordings to work through if you want to listen to me talk about it as well! You can access those (along with the other supplementary resources for this book) at: https://creativeacademyforwriters.com/resources/createstoryconflict

I'm a rule follower. I like to-do lists. I like checking things off. However, hold on to your hats—there are no rules with this book. I've written with the idea that you'll read it from front to back, but if you are the kind of rebel who likes to skip around, I won't stop you. (However, if you are the kind of person who skips to the end of the novel to read the conclusion first, I will reserve a tiny smidge of judgment. But I promise to keep it to myself.) You may enjoy reading through the book first and then going back to complete only the exercises that work for you. Or you might be the kind of person who will break this book into chunks and tackle what is most important to you at the moment. If some exercises feel pointless to you, consider yourself free from any obligation to complete them. However, in the interests of challenging you to grow, I would ask that before you skip something, take a moment to think about *why* your instinct is to skip it.

Throughout the book I discuss different aspects of conflict and then provide "Your Turn" sections where you can apply that topic or idea to your own writing. Between you and me, these prompts are where the real value lies.

As one who owns about one zillionty—this is a technical math term I made up—writing craft books, I know they serve two purposes. Both purposes are useful, but one is significantly more beneficial. The first value of a craft book is to introduce you to a concept or, in many cases, remind you of a concept. The second value, however, is to give you the opportunity put that concept into action. You apply it to your writing, and in the course of using it, you'll discover what changes it can make to your creative process and manuscript. Thinking about stuff is good—doing things is better.

Freak-out warning!

Do not panic that there is more work to do than you could ever complete. You do not need to do every single exercise in this book, and I'm certain that some won't seem to work for you at all. I promise I will not be checking your homework.

This is where we'll work together. I've provided a lot of prompts; you decide which are meaningful for *you* and *your* work and *your* process. My suggestion is to read through this book and flag the prompts that seem interesting to you, that light up that tiny spark in your brain that goes "oooh." My goal with this book is more spark and more *oooh*. No *ugh*.

My hope is that this book will be on your craft shelf for years to come, and that as you work on different manuscripts, you will dip back in, finding new things that resonate at different times. If you have any suggestions on conflict topics that I didn't include but should, please reach out to me at eileen@creativeacademyforwriters.com

Now roll up your sleeves, and let's get ready to rumble…

conflict = friction

1

WHAT IS CONFLICT?

Conflict, at its core, is friction. It's difference and disagreements. It's the thing or person, including ourselves, that keeps us from what we want. It's the thing stopping us from running full speed toward the goal we've set. It ranges from annoyance to hostility. The conflict might come from the environment, from a difference in values, from society at large, or from another person.

There are those of us who love the challenge that comes with conflict, and others who tend to run in the opposite direction when we see it coming. However, there is no getting away from the fact that life is full of conflict.

And fiction without conflict falls flat.

When I speak to agents and editors, the number one thing they find missing in manuscripts is sufficient tension. Teaching and mentoring other writers has shown me that the areas most writers struggle with are (tension) and conflict. There are reasons for this, which I'll discuss in more detail later in the book.

When I read a book and find myself able to put it down and walk away, it's often because I don't care what's happening. The conflict is either missing from the pages or the story has no personal stakes. There may be interesting characters, beautiful settings and amazing sentences, but it still feels flat. I don't feel "caught" in the story. In most cases, you simply don't have a novel if you don't have conflict.

This is usually when someone will point to a novel, most commonly in the literary genre, that is best described as a "slice of life." *Aha!* They declare. *This book doesn't have very much conflict, so there!* There is little conflict on the page, but even in these books, there is still a degree of friction. It may not be the kind of conflict that you would see in a more commercial novel, but there is still *something* getting in the character's way. However, the kind of conflict that shows up in a book you're reading may not be the kind of conflict you need for your own manuscript.

When we talk about conflict, we might not mean the same thing

Conflict isn't a one-size-fits-all issue. You'll see later in this book that it includes both external and internal options, and what works well in one story may not work well in another. Just because there is opposition in a story doesn't mean that the story will automatically be better. One mistake people make, when they're told their book doesn't have enough conflict, is throwing everything in. They think, what the heck, let's give the character a flat tire, a natural disaster and an evil overlord bent on their personal destruction. Then they wonder why it doesn't seem to be fixing the problem. They throw up their hands in frustration. They put in conflict so what's wrong now?

But conflict isn't there so you can tick a box and say you have it. The point of the conflict is to push the character, and the story, forward. *It's conflict with a purpose.*

Different genres use conflict differently. A high-action thriller will almost certainly include some kind of physical conflict—a gunfight or race through a city. A murder mystery will have a body count, but a romance novel may confine the conflict to raised voices or internal will-I-won't-I debates.

Writing an externally focused conflict requires different skills than writing a conflict that is primarily internal. (Although if it is a romantic comedy, there is a high probability of a chase scene in which one character races across the city to the airport so they can declare their love before the other character flies away. Why do these people never have a cell phone?)

In many cases, you'll be balancing elements of both internal and external conflict in your story. Your character will encounter events, characters and things in the real world that prevent them from reaching their goal, but these are made worse by the turmoil inside the character.

As a writer you need to know what kind of conflict you have in your novel and how different kinds of conflict build and look on the page. Fundamentally, there needs to be something in the way of your character, friction between them and their goal, a challenge for them to overcome (assuming you want a happy ending) or a challenge that will ultimately best them (sad ending).

Explore how other storytellers have used conflict in their work. Learning to identify conflict and its role in the story will help you develop your own manuscript. The more you do this, the more easily you will spot it and see how it makes a difference to the story. Note your own emotional reaction when something gets in the way of the character, and see how it pulls you deeper into the story. There's a reason many writers end a chapter—or the scene before a commercial on a TV show—with a new complication. It makes you turn the page (or keep watching the show) to see what the character will do next.

Your Turn

- I firmly believe that one of the best ways for writers to improve their craft is to be careful readers. Take the time to reread one of your favourite books. In every chapter, attempt to identify the conflict and use sticky notes or a highlighter to mark those conflicts. (I know some people believe marking up books is a great sin. What can I say? I'm a rebel.) When you've finished reading, go back through the conflicts again. Put a check mark if they are external conflicts and a star if they are internal. Lastly, look at how the conflict builds in the story, and how it impacts the character and the plot.

- You can also do this exercise with movies, TV dramas, half-hour sitcoms and, in some cases, commercials. Stories come in all shapes and sizes, so be open to exploring conflict in all forms.

- Listen when people tell stories about what happened to them. These may be work issues, a car breakdown, an interaction with a spouse or what happened on their vacation. How many of these stories include some kind of conflict? How does that impact your interest in hearing what happened?

Why is conflict so important in fiction?

Story *is* conflict. When you distill fiction, it's ultimately reduced to a story about an individual (character) who wants something (goal) for a good reason (motivation), and then something or someone gets in the way. That thing in the way is conflict. If you take conflict out of the equation, then you've got a character who wants something and then gets it.

Insert yawn here.

There is no tension in seeing someone want something and get it. The individual simply states a desire and then obtains it. This would be great in real life. *Hey, Universe. I would like to win the lotto, or find love, or find love and win the lotto.* (If the universe is paying attention to these desires, I feel I should get extra credit for putting them into a book.)

Before you get upset, I know the value of intentions. Trust me. I like them. I use them. (If you'd like to learn how changing the point of view of an intention can impact results—*I will be a better writer* versus *You will be a better writer*—be sure to check out *Scrappy Rough Draft by Donna Barker*.) However, as someone who has more self-help books than a Kardashian has makeup, I know that stating the intention is just the beginning. You then have to *pursue* what you want and—here's the tricky part—get back up when the universe knocks you down. Part of the satisfaction of obtaining something is working hard to obtain it.

A character who achieves their goal without effort isn't interesting. And the one thing you don't want on the page is boredom. Intention isn't action. The reader will want to see the character doing more than wishing for something. They will want to see them doing something to get it.

Readers are cruel masters. They want to see your character struggle. More, they want to see your character slog through miles of pain and hardship, crawling through broken glass. They want to see the character get knocked down, pick themselves back up and then get whacked upside the head all over again. They want to see your character backed into a corner that seems so bleak, so impossible, that they have no idea how they will ever get out of it.

Does this mean readers are psychopaths?

Maybe a few. However, the rest of us want to see that kind of struggle because we want to share that moment of victory when the character does get themselves out of that impossible situation. It gives us a touch of hope. If that character can survive—and even thrive—despite those odds, it means we might too. Think about that for a second. Your book, your character's conflict, is an opportunity to breathe hope into someone else. Pretty powerful stuff.

> *"One day, in retrospect, the years of struggle will strike you as the most beautiful."*
>
> *– Sigmund Freud*

I worked as a counsellor for over twenty years, so allow me to strap on my psychology hat for a moment. One thing that psychologists know is that conflict is a large part of what defines us as people. Struggle shapes our characters. When we reflect on our lives, we tend to think about what we needed to do to obtain the things we wanted in life. We're proud of ourselves when we get through difficult times. Often, when we look through our past, we changed and grew the most when we were responding to a difficult situation such as a death or divorce.

From the outside, we want to see who people are when things are challenging, because that struggle reveals character. It's easier to be a good person when things are going your way. When things go wrong, the mask we wear

—the image we want to project—often slips, exposing our true nature. Good or bad.

An individual's ability to get through a challenge is what matters when they look back. It isn't uncommon for people who have achieved it all to talk fondly about the time when they didn't have much of anything. A billionaire will talk wistfully about the days when he had nothing but an idea no one believed in, and the ability to run his business out of his parents' basement. A couple who has raised a family and retired comfortably in an all-amenities building will talk fondly about the times they had to scrounge for quarters in the sofa cushions in order to get laundry done. They remember mowing the lawn with one kid strapped to their back and the other in a playpen on the back deck. You barely have your diploma in your hand before you start talking nostalgically about the all-nighters you pulled, the three jobs your worked to avoid taking out another student loan, and that time you thought Jägermeister and Coke sounded like a great combination. In the moment, those were horrible experiences. (Trust me on the Jag and Coke.) But looking back, the fact you survived feels like a badge of honour. If you had sailed through as a genius trust fund baby without any need to struggle, you wouldn't have that badge.

When we look back on a conflict or struggle that we survived, we feel proud of ourselves. We have an appreciation of what we achieved. This may contribute to why readers like to see a character struggle. We sense they will survive (to save the planet, defeat the zombies, win love or find the magical dragon) and we want to be with them during the struggle so we can celebrate at the end. The harder the struggle, the bigger the celebration.

Conflict reveals character. It is easy to say you're a good person, but when it feels like everything is against you, when your back is against the wall, it allows you a chance to see "who you really are." You've likely heard the advice that you never really know who you can count on until you are in a difficult situation. Putting your character in a high-conflict situation allows them to shine and step up— or fail.

It may be useful here to point out that you can use conflict to show a character who doesn't succeed. It might be a secondary character facing the same obstacle as your protagonist. If the secondary character is unable to meet the challenge, it can provide a contrast and a cautionary tale for the reader.

Readers want to *know* your characters. Conflict gives deeper insight into the characters and can result in readers caring even more about them. The more empathy that a reader has for a character, the more engaged they are in the story. Science is going to back me up on this. Empathy releases oxytocin in the brain. Oxytocin is sometimes referred to as the "love hormone." When you want a reader to love a book or a character, eliciting their empathy is one way to reach that goal.

Yes! You are impacting the brain chemistry of people with your words. (Pro tip: Try not to go mad with this power.)

Not knowing what will happen to a character creates tension. Think of a series of conflicts stretching through your book like a tight cord, a tow rope that pulls the reader through to the final page. They want to see how the character will navigate these choppy waters, and they will turn pages and read "just one more chapter" in order to discover what happens next.

Tension also needs to be alleviated. The reader wants the rubber band to snap, wants to get it over with, in the same way they want a ticking rollercoaster to just start going downhill already. We can't stay in that place of upheaval. We will read to see what happens and to get some relief.

If you really want to torture readers—and really, what other source of fun do we have as writers?—end your chapters where it seems the tension will break, but then ratchet it higher. *Oh, ho, ho, you thought you would go to bed after reading this chapter, did you? Forget it. You're going to be up until 2:00 a.m., and I don't give a damn that you have work, school, a meeting, a flight to catch, or anything else to do tomorrow.* (Insert your own maniacal laughter here.) And yes, it *is* ironic that I called some readers psychopaths earlier in this section.

Your Turn

- Journal about a time you were under a lot of pressure or facing a lot of conflict. How did you behave or respond? What did your response show about your character?
- Journal about a time someone you knew was in a difficult situation. Did they respond well or

poorly? Were you ever shocked by what you learned about that individual?

- Is there a struggle that your character looks back on fondly, impressed with what they got through? Conversely, is there something in their past they aren't proud of?

TYPES OF CONFLICT—EXTERNAL CONFLICT

There are primarily two kinds of conflict in fiction: external and internal. External conflict is anything in the world that opposes your character. This might be another person, a group of people, society as a whole, a systemic issue, weather, nature in general (bears can cause a lot of trouble) or anything else you can think to throw at them.

Internal conflict is the opposite. It's what is happening inside your character that keeps them from pursuing their goal. You've likely heard the term "your own worst enemy," which summarizes internal conflict rather succinctly and is the reason so many of us end up in some form of therapy.

If you want to watch a few writers duke it out, raise the argument that commercial fiction typically features only external conflict, while in literary fiction the only source of conflict is internal. (If you haven't been to a fancy writer party, this is the kind of thing that brings the excitement.

That and watching a group of introverts try to socialize with real people versus their imaginary friends.) While there may be some stories that embody this narrow theory, there are plenty of books, both commercial and literary, that don't. Most writers agree the more the merrier with conflict, so most novels have both, external and internal, although the driving conflict may lean one way or the other.

Neither source of conflict is better than the other. There's often a desire among writers to know the "right" answer so they can write a book and be published. But the truth is that when it comes to plotting a story, writing dialogue or following a writing process, there aren't these absolutes. Where you choose to put the emphasis in your conflict will likely come from your story and what interests you as a writer.

Your Turn

- Does your manuscript have external conflict? What kind?
- Does your manuscript have internal conflict? What are the things at war within the character?
- Perhaps your book has a bit of both types of conflict. If there is only one, is there an opportunity to add some more? (Never fear—I'm going to give you some ideas below.)

Sources of external conflict

External conflict is what happens in the world to prevent your character from reaching their goal. Whenever it feels like the world is out to get you, you're troubled by external conflict. (You may also be paranoid, but that's a separate problem.)

The beauty of external conflict is that the character, as well as the reader, can see, hear and experience it. It isn't a state of mind; it is something or someone that is actually in the way. And if we can see what is in the way, we can see how the character will get around (or through) it. Unlike something internal, progress against an external conflict is easier to measure and track.

Let's take a closer look at a few external things that may get in the way of your character, and then explore how you can use them in a book.

Weather and nature

Ever have one of those days? You're running late. You need to get to work for an important meeting, but first you have to walk the dogs because otherwise, there's no way they'll make it all day without destroying something. You step outside, and it's raining. Not a nice, soft spring drizzle, but the kind of cold, driving rain that feels like a million tiny ice arrows stabbing your face. The dogs aren't cooperating. Instead of getting down to business, they are intent on sniffing every square inch of ground, pausing to savour each scent as if they were a sommelier in a high-end restaurant and each puddle were a rare bottle of

Bordeaux. The wind is blowing hard enough that you look like a reporter calling in during a hurricane update on the evening news. A car drives through a puddle, drenching you in freezing, muddy water.

Wait, what's that? Oh God, there is an actual *worm* in your hair. It must have come from the puddle. There's something wrong with the worm—it's half-squished, and internal worm bits are coming out. You have a terminally ill worm in your hair and no way to get it out because you don't have a Kleenex and you don't want to use your hands. You're still running late, and you'll have to go to work with your hair looking like a worm war zone, and it can't get any worse.

That's when you step in a pile of still-warm dog poop.

That's an example of nature ruining your day. And we haven't even gotten to tornados, fire or plague. Not to mention zombies or being eaten by bears. Nature frequently wreaks havoc in our lives. At times, this is on a grand scale (see tornados, bears, or bear-nados. Someone call Netflix, that's a winner idea!). Other times, it's just an annoyance (rain), but in both cases, it throws up roadblocks to your character's forward movement.

If you're writing a historical novel, then nature is an even larger factor to consider. In the 1800s, if a fire took out your food stores, starving was a real possibility because there wasn't a local Trader Joe's down the block. Winter was long, and Costco wasn't a thing. Travel required traversing large open areas where you were often at the whim of nature. (Think about that Donner party dining on each other in the frozen mountains of the Sierra Nevada—

imagine what they would have done for a Trader Joe's, if for nothing else than a good barbecue sauce to go on top of Uncle Pete.)

In fantasy novels, you will have created a natural system with all its risks. Perhaps... winter is coming. (I've been waiting to use that in a sentence for some time.) There may be unique creatures, dragons or spider-bear crossbreeds for example, that a character needs to worry about. There may be black rain that's toxic, a flower that can be used for magical purposes or trees that leap to life and move about on their own.

In space, there are black holes, a freezing cold atmosphere, and out-of-control satellites to consider. Andy Weir's runaway bestseller *The Martian* is an excellent example of man versus nature. The main character, Mark Watney, is abandoned on Mars after a freak windstorm. He struggles to stay alive in one of the most hostile environments known to man. If you weren't cheering for him to grow potatoes and figure out how to recycle urine, then I don't understand you.

Even in contemporary novels, nature can create a challenge. This may be because your main character's plane crashes in a remote corner of the Yukon, leaving them nothing more than one stale granola bar, a pair of Ugg boots, a spoon, and a now-cold Starbucks soy-no-sugar vanilla latte in order to survive. You may also use nature as a minor annoyance, such as unexpected rain on the day your character was planning an outdoor wedding, wind that blows away a vital clue in a mystery, or the always unpleasant dog poop on the shoe.

Your Turn

- Do you have any nature conflicts in your story? If not, is there room to add to conflict by making the world around your character turn against them?
- If you're writing a historical novel, have you researched to see if any major weather events occurred during the time your story covers?
- If you're writing a fantasy or science-fiction novel, have you determined how nature functions in this new world? Are there rules?
- How does the weather support your story or theme?

Social and systemic conflict

Another source of external conflict is society at large, where your character is at odds with the dominant culture. This may pose a major or minor problem depending on your character and the society in which they operate. If you are writing about an African American living in the South during the Civil War, there are significant systemic issues and challenges they will have to face in order to pursue their goal. If you are writing about an unpopular student in school, they may have to cope with a very rigid social structure. A maid in *Downton Abbey* faced different challenges than the lady of the manor. The degree of conflict depends on the situation.

We all exist within a larger society, and we either fit in, or we don't. We are either at the top of the food chain or not, and you need to know your character's place in the hierarchy. It's also interesting to reflect on how aware of their status your character is. Is their perception correct or not?

If you are writing a story in which your character is an underdog in a system stacked against them, there will be systemic or societal conflict. Perhaps you've had this experience personally because you come from a marginalized group and have had to fight harder than someone with the benefit of being privileged.

Ever try fighting the system? It isn't easy. Systems are solid, slow and hard to move. As a dual citizen, I have two passports. (I'm like a super spy.) I was told that when I entered the United States, I was required to use my US passport. As a Canadian entering Canada, I was supposed to use my Canadian passport. However, I was told not to use different passports for coming and going.

Anyone else see the problem here?

I spent hours on the phone with various customs and border officials trying to resolve this issue, but as anyone who has ever tried to fight the law has discovered, it doesn't matter if the system doesn't make sense—the law wins. (Please don't turn me in to border patrol or start singing that annoying song.)

If you are writing fantasy or speculative fiction, be aware that you will need to do some world-building to explain the social structure. You must clarify the cultural expectations and just exactly how your character does or doesn't fit into the mould of what is expected.

Keep in mind that within a larger society, there are sub-societies like a school, a social club or a family. Perhaps you are the fifth generation in a family that has owned a hardware business. The expectation is that you will take on that family business and run it in a way consistent with how it's been run before. But perhaps you want to run it differently. Perhaps you want to include a book section—can you tell I've always dreamed of running a bookstore?—and the family has strong feelings about that. Or perhaps—oh, the horror!—you don't want to be in the hardware business at all. Another example would be that your family may prize athletic skills, complete with family football games for the holidays, and you have zero coordination.

You may also have a character who used to fit quite well into their society, but then something happened. Perhaps they saw something that changed their perspective, or something happened to them that has suddenly put them at odds. The people around them will want them to "return to the fold" and not to "rock the boat." (And your editor will want you to find non-clichéd ways to describe this problem.) Perhaps your character was a part of the popular crowd at school. Because of a class project, they've become friends with someone outside the inner circle. Will they choose their new friend or ignore them?

Tackling society can be a challenge. Many writers create a specific character that is a stand-in for that system—a slave owner, a Darth Vader, a snotty popular cheerleader. This allows things to become personal for the main character. It's not them against a large system, it's them against a particular person. A character such as Darth Vader becomes a symbol of the Empire and everything wrong with that system. Vader is cold and calculating. He favours power for a select few at a cost to the many. He is corrupt and evil. Those same terms also describe the Empire, a bloated intergalactic government that has seriously lost its way.

Hating a large system can be hard. Hating an individual is much easier.

Your Turn

- What is the society within which your character functions? (Consider the overarching one, but also the smaller "sub-societies" they are a part of.)
- List the rules of the society in your manuscript. Next to each rule (which may be unspoken), indicate if your main character agrees with it or not.
- What beliefs and values does the society hold? What do they see as important? Later in this book, we'll be discussing character values, so there may be an opportunity to put character and society values in conflict.

Setting

This can be similar to nature, but it's worth a look on its own as there are differences. It is also an area of the writing craft that is often under-utilized. Many writers limit setting to an objective description of what surrounds the characters. The office contains a desk, lamp and chair. The wall is covered in bookcases. The walls are painted white and have a collection of brightly coloured modern art prints. That description may be accurate, but it's not necessarily interesting. It doesn't make me feel anything or tell me anything about the people using that space. Don't think of setting as just the "set" upon which the story takes place. Think about how that setting can reinforce other things in your story including theme, tone—and conflict.

If you have any doubts about this, talk to someone in the film industry who works in the area of set decoration. If you thought they just looked around and grabbed what was handy to fill the space, you have no idea how much thought goes into everything from the cushion on the sofa to the choice of wallpaper. They use the set—colour, texture and all the tiny details—to reinforce character and tone and to enhance the conflict in the scene. In the office description above, they might make the walls stark white and the prints disturbing shades of red and black. The desk might be old, carved, with lots of tiny cubbyholes and heavy locks that look like they are holding something in instead of keeping curious people out. The bookcase might be shot from an angle that makes it loom over the person in the chair. All of a sudden, the space feels foreboding and even a touch creepy.

Space and setting can make someone feel comfortable or
uneasy. If you describe a creepy basement, complete with
cobwebs, abandoned and rusted tools, and a pit dug out of
the earth, pretty much no one will want to spend a lot of
time there. Because I'm an introvert, something that is
certain to make my palms sweat and my heart race is
walking into a social event where I don't know anyone.
You can count on me to bring up random and
inappropriate small talk—*Hey, did you know more people are
killed by cows than shark attacks?* (True, by the way)—and
start my quirky snort-laugh. If you want to increase
tension and the chance for conflict, place me in a scene
with a party. One that requires shapewear and heels. Heck,
I might find this more frightening than the serial killer
basement.

This example shows that conflict may come not from the
setting per se, but from an individual's comfort within that
setting. I have a small (understatement) dental phobia. As
soon as I walk into the office, my heart beats faster and I
get that smear of oily sweat across my chest and in my
underarms. The smell of a dental office is enough to put
me on edge. One glance at the tidy display of torture
implements makes me want to run. If I hear that drill, even
if they are drilling some other poor soul, I want to
throw up.

A good friend of mine loves the dentist. She naps while
they clean her teeth. *Naps.* As in, she is so relaxed that she
drifts off to sleep. She feels no stress. Many people work
every day in dental offices and don't have panic attacks
doing it. I can barely manage to go for an hour every six
months without a meltdown, but others basically hang out

there. Other settings that upset some people but not others include office buildings, cars, your accountant's office, the country, a downtown street and your in-laws' house, complete with copious tiny, breakable items precariously placed on every surface.

Some settings are predisposed to conflict. They are places where stress is high (airports, hospitals) or where people's expectations can differ (Disneyland, furniture stores). Did you know that IKEA used to employ store counsellors to help people who had broken down in their attempt to assemble furniture they couldn't pronounce? As a writer, you can enjoy a good, long airport layover. Plop yourself down in a seat with a good view, and watch humanity go by. I can almost promise you'll have the opportunity to view conflict.

Just remember that characters who are comfortable are less likely to engage in conflict or react in a negative way than characters who feel out of place or stressed.

Your Turn

- What is the first thing that comes to your mind when you think of a place where your character would feel most comfortable? Least comfortable?
- Look at the scene settings in your novel. Are there any you could change to maximize the conflict?
- Consider how descriptions of a setting change the feel. Take five to ten minutes to describe the space you are in at the moment. Then take another five to ten minutes to describe the same space, but

imagine you're writing a horror novel. Then take yet another five or ten minutes and describe the setting through the eyes of someone who has time-travelled to that space from the 1700s. What things would someone in a horror novel notice—the looming bookcase, threatening to bury them alive? What would the time traveller notice—the odd flame-free device that gives off no heat but is still so bright?

- How could changing the setting in your novel make things worse for your character or increase the opportunity for conflict?
- Look at the sensory details in a place that makes them uncomfortable. How can you highlight these? What are the smells and textures?
- Is your character in a relationship with someone who feels exactly the opposite in that setting?

Working with my enemy

An interesting form of external conflict results when your character must partner with their enemies. You may have heard the quote "the enemy of my enemy is my friend." There are times when groups or individuals have to join forces with someone they typically dislike in order to beat a common foe.

You can see this dynamic in everything from the US and Russia joining forces in World War II to the cast of misfits in Marvel's *Guardians of the Galaxy*. A conservative religious organization may join forces with a feminist one in order to protest pornography together.

The challenge, and fun, of this scenario is the opportunity to create conflict between people who are on the same team. How will they navigate the challenges that typically keep them apart? What will they learn about each other?

A bad guy (or creature)

At long last, we've come to the most common external conflict source—the bad guy, the one character the reader loves to hate. This is the character who wants to thwart your main character in the pursuit of their goal.

Let's hear it for the Wicked Witches, the Voldemorts, the Hannibal Lecters, the evil counts, the aliens and the jerks named Todd in human resources, who get in the way of our characters' goals. Readers often enjoy reading scenes with these characters the most. There's something delicious about a great bad guy or girl. They often say or do the things that we would never do—but perhaps have occasionally wanted to do. Writers also admit that writing the bad guy can be a lot of fun.

As I mentioned above, your bad guy or gal may be a placeholder for a society or system that is corrupt, but they still need to be well-rounded. It helps to remember that the bad guy often doesn't know they are the bad guy. As far as they're concerned, they're the hero of the story. Your villain should want to get in the way of your main character for a *really* good reason. The fact that you need a bad guy is not a good enough reason for the reader. The bad guy needs a strong motivation. They will push forward to reach their individual goals if you sufficiently motivate them. If the bad guy just randomly causes trouble, it feels weak to the reader. Sure, there are people who just cause trouble. But they're not that interesting. The villains that really suck readers in are those that have their own code, their own reasons, for the actions they take. It may be a seriously messed-up ethical code, but to the reader it is intriguing to understand that.

It is often the relationship between the bad guy and the protagonist that makes for interesting reading. Sherlock Holmes is pushed to be a better character because he faces Moriarty. It's not an accident that Darth Vader turns out to be Luke Skywalker's dad. That makes it that much worse for Luke. (And he was already having a bad day even before dear old Dad cut off his hand. Talk about a need for some serious family therapy, and we haven't even touched on Luke's weird relationship with his sister.) You want to consider not only that you have a bad guy in your book, but that he's the *best* nemesis for your main character. If you're seeking help with how to craft your bad guy, consider the book *Characters, Emotion & Viewpoint* by Nancy Kress as a good resource.

Your protagonist and bad guy may not even be on opposing sides. It's possible that they both want the same thing, but what they are willing to do to obtain that thing will put them on a collision course.

Your Turn

- Why does your bad guy want to stop your main character? What is it that they want in the book and why do they want it? Are there people who would agree with them?
- Write a journal entry from your villain's point of view that explains what they find annoying, challenging, or rage-inducing about your character.
- Pull out some of your favourite books and look at the bad guy (or girl). What makes them interesting?
- If you were to turn your story upside down—the way *Wicked* tells the *Wizard of Oz* from the Wicked Witch's perspective—how would your bad guy tell the story?

A good guy (or creature) who wants the same as your character

This is a variation of the option above, but it's worth a mention. Sometimes the person who gets in your main character's way isn't a bad guy. They might be a good guy, or even your main character's best friend. They simply want the same thing.

Imagine you are writing a book where the main character wants to win a dance competition. It's very important because the first prize in the competition is a scholarship and without these funds, they won't be able to pay for school. Let's also add in some strong emotion: the character's mom was a dancer, and—before she was tragically diagnosed with some awful disease that has given her only pages (or weeks) to live—she always dreamed of her daughter following in her footsteps.

The competition is going to come down to your main character and their very best friend, the one they grew up with, practically as sisters. Unfortunately, this BFF *also* needs to win the competition for a really good reason. It might be a bit of coincidence if her mother also was dying, so instead we'll say that her family is being held hostage by terrorists who, for reasons that are unclear, also require her to win the contest.

They both can't win the contest. They both have really good (although perhaps not really plausible) motivations for winning. Conflict between these two ensues. It's important to keep this idea of a good guy in mind because it's easy to default to the belief that there must be a bad guy—even though being in conflict with someone you are close to, someone who really matters, can be much more difficult.

In romance, consider a woman who has a crush on someone her friend also has a crush on. Alternate relationship situations notwithstanding, in most cases both of these women can't obtain the object of their desire. This is the premise behind *Cyrano de Bergerac* (and the Steve Martin movie *Roxanne*). A man loves the beautiful Roxanne but helps another win her hand instead.

Your Turn

- Consider a time in your life when a friend or family member was in pursuit of the same thing you were. How did you feel?
- Would it be worse for your character to be opposed by someone they normally go to for support?
- Is there a character in your book who would normally be on their side, but in this instance—this very, very, very important instance—is on the opposite side?

Make them worthy of your protagonist

If your main character is set up in a conflict with a person (or place or thing) that is weak, it makes your protagonist look weak. I mentioned this above when talking about the villain, but it's important in all cases. If your main character goes up against someone or something who is their equal (or heck, their better) in strength, it gives the reader more to cheer for when the character triumphs. No one is impressed if a lion beats a mouse. That's the way we expect it to work out. A lion going after a mouse isn't a conflict that will keep people on the edge of their seat. Now, if the mouse gets crafty—perhaps he has a concealed carry permit and ends up besting the lion—*that's* interesting.

Consider Episode IV of the first Star Wars movies. (I firmly believe George Lucas numbered them this way to drive me crazy.) In this film, we're introduced to Luke Skywalker. He's a farmer. A moisture farmer, if you can imagine anything more mind-numbingly dull. He has to go up against Darth Vader, who, say what you will about his moral compass, is clearly a badass. Vader has a better outfit, better weapons and an awesome James Earl Jones voice.

At the end of the film, when Luke has to attempt to blow up the Death Star, it's the first time he's ever piloted a fighter jet. He's behind the wheel of a highly complex X-wing fighter. He makes a comment about how it's just like the landspeeder he used to chase down womp rats on Tatooine.

Ponder that for a moment. Imagine that you are a well-trained rebellion leader, and the only guy left who might save the day is a moisture farmer who hasn't a clue what he's doing. Feeling good about the good guys' chances? Yeah, not so much.

A mismatched protagonist makes the reader (or viewer) even more happy when they succeed despite the odds. This means that the more skills you give your main character, the more you need to give to your antagonist as well. If your protagonist has too many advantages over the antagonist, the reader will lose their desire to cheer them on. They will expect your hero to win, and that's just not exciting.

Your Turn

- On a scale of one to ten, where one is weak and ten is Darth Vader–level badassery, where does your antagonist fall? Are they bad enough to make your protagonist really have to stretch in order to be successful?
- Create a list of your protagonist's strengths and weaknesses. Then list your antagonist's strengths and weaknesses. How well-matched are they? In what situations is one stronger than the other? Is there a way that your antagonist can be extra strong in a way your protagonist is extra weak?

TYPES OF CONFLICT- INTERNAL CONFLICT

Many of us know (internal conflict) all too well. It's the battle inside as different elements push and pull us toward and away from what we want. There are two primary sources of internal conflict.

Competing wants

Ever want to eat healthier *and* eat the cookie at the same time? (Please don't let this just be me.) That is internal conflict. When you want to put your family first *and* focus on your passion. When you want to work on your writing craft *and* watch Netflix for hours straight until it asks, "Are you still watching?" in that slightly judgmental tone.

Competing wants are a common source of internal conflict. Donald Maass's book *Writing the Breakout Novel* has one of my favourite exercises. It asks you to list what your character wants. Then it asks you to think of the opposite of that want and determine how your character can want both of those things at the same time. At first this exercise seemed impossible to me; how could someone want opposite things? But the more I did the exercise, the more it occurred to me how fundamental this truth was, and how often I found myself in the same dilemma. Without a competing want, it is much easier to reach your goal. You simply state what you want and then move toward it. But when those wants are in conflict, we are more challenged to reach our target.

Your Turn

Consider a past goal that was difficult to reach or that you abandoned. What stopped you from reaching that goal? Were any of these obstacles internal? Did you use an external obstacle as an excuse? What competing wants did you face? For example, if your goal was to complete university and you dropped out, was it because your parents refused to pay for school if you pursued something "silly" like creative writing? That's an external reason. But if you dig deep, there were ways around this barrier. You could have changed majors. You could have taken out loans. You could have worked part time and gone to school part time. What was happening internally that kept you from trying one of these alternatives? The goal of this exercise isn't to beat yourself up or make yourself feel bad. (Or to drive you into therapy, for that matter). The goal is to recognize that what often prevents us from reaching our goals is what we tell ourselves.

- What is the primary goal that drives your character? What competing wants might they have? How can you show these in your manuscript?
  - Does your character acknowledge these competing wants, or are they in denial?
  - Is your character able to identify both external and internal impacts on their goal?
- What does your character's inner voice tell them about what they want? Does it whisper "you've got this" or "you'll never amount to anything"?

Values and beliefs

Values are deeply held beliefs that drive your actions and reactions. They help you determine what is important to you and assist you in setting priorities in your life. Most of our values are shaped in childhood by our family, which sets guidelines about what is important or not. For example, I can remember running errands with my dad as a kid. We had gotten home when he realized that he had been given too much change at the store. And I'm talking *change*—a nickel, as I recall. My dad piled me back into the car and we went back to the store, through cross-town traffic, to return the coin. My dad told me it wasn't his money to keep and that it was important to be honest. That stuck with me. This idea of honesty was reinforced over and over in our family.

I also recalled getting spanked for telling a lie. I'd been playing out by the street in front of my house, floating orange peels in the gutter after a rainy spell. (What can I say? This was before cable TV). My dad pulled into the driveway, and I ran into the house because I was forbidden from playing so close to the street.

My dad came in and asked me if I had been out by the road. I remember thinking vaguely that if he was asking a question, maybe he didn't know for sure. So I lied. "Nope, wasn't me." He then paddled me, not because I'd been playing in the road (at least that was the official story) but because I'd lied.

It could be that my dad watched too many John Wayne movies, or perhaps he inherited the value from his parents, but honesty was highly prized in our home. There was a lot of discussion about how giving someone your word mattered deeply—how it was a bond. To this day, one of the things I struggle with most is when someone lies to me. It's a deal breaker.

Another value that was strong in our home was the virtue of being on time. I was raised with the idea that not being on time was disrespecting the other person. I have a deep aversion to not being punctual. As a result, if you invite me over you can almost bet that I'll be twenty to thirty minutes early and parked outside your house like a creeper holding the bottle of wine I brought. (But not so creepy that I'm sitting out there drinking it while watching you through a window.) There is a reason I never leave the house without a book or something else to read—it's because I know I'll have plenty of time to read a few pages.

But there have been times in my life when I've lied. Perhaps I felt that another value—kindness, for example—took precedent. I may have felt that I had no choice but to lie. Or I may have been too weak to face the consequences of being honest. There have also been times when I've continued doing something I felt was really important, even knowing that it might make me late. But any time I've acted in opposition to one of my values, it's caused internal conflict.

Values are also tricky. Some stay constant over the course of our lives, and others may change. Depending on what is happening in our life, a value that we had held dear for years may suddenly seem less important. This may be a slow evolution or the result of a single event that completely changes how we see the world.

We act on our values all the time. I used to do career counselling, and I looked at a client's values in addition to their interests, skills, abilities and education. If someone has a job that contrasts with their values, they will have a high level of dissatisfaction and likely not remain long in that role. Remember when I mentioned honesty was important to me? My first job after graduating university was selling private education to individuals. It involved heavy sales. We were told it didn't matter if we thought the clients were ill-suited to the education, if we thought they wouldn't be employed after they completed the training, or even if we thought they wouldn't complete the training. What mattered was selling a seat in that class and getting their money.

I didn't last long. I used to throw up on Monday mornings when the work week was starting. The day-to-day tasks were fine. I enjoyed meeting with people. The paperwork wasn't complicated. The office was nice. But I hated that job. I felt slimy and dishonest. I had a values conflict.

Need more examples of values clash? Someone might value honesty, but if their child is starving and they have no funds, they might consider stealing. Someone might value independence, but if it means giving up a relationship they want, they may change their mind. Success may drive an individual for the majority of their life, but faced with a new baby, they may decide that economic success needs to take a back seat. Value shifting, like any change, is often difficult and rarely a one-time event.

Your Turn

- Make a list of your character's values. If you need some suggestions, consider the list below, which can also be downloaded as a PDF resource from: https://creativeacademyforwriters.com/resources/CreateStoryConflict
- Choose five of these for your character. Select three as the most important to your character. Consider where each of those values came from, and what happened to your character to make them embrace those values as central to their lives. What values in this list are unimportant to them? What are their family values? Friends' values?

Authenticity

Adventure

Authority

Autonomy

Balance

Beauty

Boldness

Bravery

Calm

Compassion

Community

Common Sense

Creativity

Curiosity

Dignity

Equality

Fairness

Faith

Fame

Family

Friendships

Freedom

Fun

Growth

Happiness

Honesty

Honour

Independence

Justice

Kindness

Knowledge

Leadership

Learning

Logic

Love

Loyalty

Openness

Optimism

Peace

Pleasure

Popularity

Recognition

Religion

Reputation

Respect

Responsibility

Security

Self-Respect

Service

Spirituality

Stability

Success

Status

Timeliness

Trustworthiness

Wealth

Wisdom

The impact of character arc

Your character may feel internal friction because they are changing as a part of their character arc in the story. Perhaps they're developing a new way of seeing the world and interacting with others. Perhaps they're learning some hard truths about themselves. Often this involves a value change.

Consider the changes your character undergoes in the story and reflect on how that feels for them. Individuals do not change easily. They tend to go back and forth as they try to put into place a new way of responding. People are rarely one-time changers. That is, in order to establish a new way of responding or seeing the world, they will try the new behaviour, then resume their old ways, try the new way again— and repeat over and over until the new behaviour sticks.

Your Turn

- Have you ever been in a situation or relationship that created a clash in your values? When did you become aware of the conflict? How did you resolve it? Dig deep, and journal on how you felt about this clash.
- What might need to happen for your character to act against their values?
- If you character is experiencing a change in their values, what is causing that change? How can you show it by going back and forth between the two values?

TENSION AND CONFLICT

The terms *tension* and *conflict* are often used interchangeably, but they do have subtle differences.

Tension might be best described as anticipation—as that moment when you know something may happen at any time, but it hasn't happened yet. Tension can exist in everything from watching the countdown on a bomb timer to waiting for a kiss from a flirtatious date.

There can be positive tension and negative tension. For example, you may be giddy about the kiss to come. Or you may notice that the individual has Dorito crumbs all over their mouth and you are about to receive a wet, nacho-cheese lip-lock that will leave you with trauma and a desire never to eat cheesy snack foods again.

Conflict is an active instance of friction. It's happening in the moment; it is not anticipatory in any way. I would argue that conflict doesn't have to be a negative thing—we often need to disagree in order to learn more about each other and work together, and in that sense it is neutral. However, conflict is rarely seen as a positive.

What conflict and tension have in common is their power to pull readers into the story to see what will happen or discover the character's reaction after the conflict or tension occurs.

Conflict and tension both tighten and loosen as the story progresses. Think of a printout of an EKG of a heartbeat, going up and down. While it might seem, because tension and conflict are good, that a writer should keep their foot on the gas, in fact the reader needs a chance to catch their breath. Think of a roller coaster. There is the slow tick, tick, tick, as the cart climbs an impossibly high hill. This is the moment of tension. You know there is no getting off, and it is usually at this point that you begin to question your life choices and wonder if that deep-fried-pickle-and-Oreo combo is going to make a reappearance at any moment.

Then the cart crests the hill and you rush downward. This is the moment of conflict. People throw their hands up in the air—hopefully the only things they throw up are their hands—and scream, releasing all the built-up tension. However, the rollercoaster isn't simply all down. There are moments where the coaster rolls around a corner. It gives you a chance to catch your breath, reaffirm that if you ever survive this ride you will never ever, ever, *ever*, do it again, and the then coaster takes off again. You need the break, if for no other reason than to fill your lungs with air so you can scream again.

Remember to leave room for your readers to get their breath of air, too.

How to build tension

Hopefully I've convinced you to create moments of tension on the page. But how do you get it there? No worries, I've got you covered.

Create an emotional connection

You need to create an emotional connection to the characters, or you're not getting the best bang for the buck with your conflict and tension. For example, in many cheesy horror movies we see a female character sitting alone in a darkened home when she hears on the radio that a deranged serial killer—often complete with knives for hands and a penchant for wanting to eat the hearts of his victims—is on the loose. The character then hears an odd noise outside. She picks up the phone, but it's not working. She leans out the door into the gloomy night. She may call out to her boyfriend, "Brian, if that's you, it's not funny. I'm scared." The odd noise happens again. Then for reasons that are unknown to anyone with a working brain cell, she walks out into the yard—often dressed in only a T-shirt and a pair of panties—to investigate. She may or may not have a "weapon" like a shoe clutched in one hand.

We all *know* something will happen to her. Either she'll be chopped up by the knife-hand dude, or a cute dog will bound out the dark and scare her, but she's not simply going to look around, see nothing, and walk back inside.

There's tension as she strolls about, flickering flashlight in hand, and we wait for the event to happen. Then she is either attacked or merely startled, and we all jump in our seats. However, in many cases we don't really care whether she gets scared by the dog or eaten by the killer.

That's not good.

It should matter whether she's chopped up or lives to wander around in her underwear again. However, if we take the time as writers to show our characters, to allow readers to get to know and care for them, then their conflict will matter more. We no longer want her to have her heart snacked on. This is why many horror films linger over the characters we're meant to care about. Those are the stories that stick with us and give us nightmares for weeks to come.

Consider when you hear about a tragedy on TV and think, "That's horrible." Then you turn the channel so you can binge-watch *Say Yes to the Dress*. However, if someone you knew or cared about was involved in that tragedy, you would be gathering all the information you could about what happened. You'd be calling family members and driving to a hospital to wait outside. This is why TV news organizations do their best to humanize tragedy. Rather than talk about how bad a hurricane was, they will interview someone digging through the wreckage to find their dog. They don't simply show an out of control fire. They show wildlife fleeing the flames, people racing through a blood-red sky with everything they could grab in a truck, trying to get away before the fire closes off the road. The more we know about a person's story, the more we will care about the conflict they are facing.

Your Turn

- Pull two or three of your favourite books off the shelf (or pick a favourite TV show or movie). Write the name of the main character at the top of the page and then a journal entry about why you care about that person.
- Imagine that you are a TV producer and you want to foster interest in a story about what happens to your main character. What would you want the audience to know in order to get them emotionally involved in the story?

Give your reader more information than you give the protagonist

Let's go back to our horror movie for a moment. Perhaps the young woman has no idea there is a serial killer on the loose. She's simply sitting inside enjoying a book and a cup of tea. Neither she nor the audience have any inkling of what's in store. That doesn't create much tension. However, if you film the scene through the serial killer's eyes (perhaps even through his hockey mask) as he creeps up to a house and watches a woman through the window, tension will build. The audience or reader wants to scream at the woman, "Don't go outside!"

Perhaps you're writing science fiction. Either an omniscient narrator, or another character, may see or show a leak in a pipe in the (insert fancy technical name for a spaceship engine here). The reader sees the gas hissing, just out of sight of our favourite character. We all know that an explosion will tear a hole in the ship and that people we like, including the roguishly cute ship doctor, will be sucked into space. A character begins to play with a lighter, and every single reader clenches their butt cheeks, waiting for the boom.

If you're writing in the first person, it is more challenging to create a situation where the main character isn't aware of something but the reader is. However, it's still possible. In order to make it work, the main character must observe, hear or experience something but create a different meaning for it than the reader does.

For example, in a romance book, the first-person protagonist, single author Ellen (work with me here) is at a swanky literary party where she meets a dashing gentleman. Let's give him an accent and a really interesting job like astronaut. I'm crazy for accents and smart men. I mean, I'm sure that's what *Ellen* likes. As Ellen describes the scene, she may have some internal thoughts about how he's dreamy, but that for whatever reason, she doesn't think he would be interested in her. (Cue a need to work on self-confidence.) But the audience reads what the sexy English astronaut has to say and concludes, "Girlfriend, he is *totally* flirting with you." It creates tension as we wonder, will Ellen sort it out? Will she get lucky, or will she go home alone and snuggle only a dog for the evening?

Your Turn

- Draw a line down the centre of a sheet of paper. On one side, write down what the main character knows in a particular scene. On the other side, show what the reader (or you, the author) knows. Is there a way to build tension by hiding something from your character?
- Fix Ellen up with a sexy science guy to see what happens. (Okay, that's not really a writing exercise, but I'm interested to hear how it turns out. Then you can write about it. It's a win-win thing. English accent not required—I'll also accept Irish, Scottish, Italian... heck, pretty much anything.)

Up the stakes

There is a whole section later in the book on the importance of stakes, so I won't go into much detail here, but it is important to understand that the more something matters to the character, the more the reader will feel tense when this thing is placed at risk.

If you character leaves their adorable shire full of happy fellow hobbits to travel through all sorts of inhospitable places and throw a ring into a fiery pit of hell, then it had better *really* matter that the ring go to that place. Otherwise the reader will think it's a pretty stupid hobbit.

Your Turn

- What is at risk for your character in the scene?
- What will happen if your character doesn't take the action they were intending to take?

Create a background for tension

When making the classic film *Jaws*, Steven Spielberg had a problem. The shark didn't work. It was a giant animatronic dud. It had a tendency to sink. He was making a movie all about a killer shark, and every time he tried to film a scene, the thing refused to work or slowly sank to the bottom of the tank. This is what is known as a Big Problem in the film industry. Money circled the drain as time went by, and cast and crew were ready to film, but… no shark.

Spielberg knew he had to come up with another solution, so he used music to add to the tension. He would show a child on an inflatable toy, tiny skinny legs jerking around in the water, and then you would hear it.

Da-duh.

Go back to the legs flailing around like meat on a stick, a kid-kabob, and show the child laughing.

Da-duh, da-duh, da-duh. (Cue growing anxiety in the audience. They quickly swallow that popcorn and grip the hand of the person they came with, or perhaps the hand of a random stranger.)

Show the little boy again, his hair adorably flopping over one eye. Perhaps he scans the beach for his mom. A cute dog playing on the beach barks out a warning.

Da-duh, da-duh, da-duh, da-duh— CHOMP.

A sad, deflated toy floats on top of the red-tinged water. The dog howls.

Spielberg contrasted the mood of the music with what was happening on screen to create a feeling of dread in the audience. Even before you knew what the music meant, you sensed that it wasn't anything good. Music is used over and over in film to cultivate a feeling. Unless you're writing an interactive book or audiobook complete with background music, you won't have the benefit of a soundtrack to cue tension in the reader. But consider what is happening in the background to add to tension. What things may show the reader that despite what is happening on the page, there is something else going on? To do this, consider your descriptions and pull in sensory details that may be early clues.

Your Turn

- Look at a scene that appears just *before* a high-conflict moment in your manuscript. Does it give the reader any clues that something may be about to happen?
- Review your sensory description in tense or conflicted scenes. Are you getting the biggest bang out of them? Instead of something smelling sour,

perhaps there is a scent of decay. Is there a noise just barely audible, almost like someone is whispering a warning?

5

WRITERS AND CONFLICT

Why do writers sometimes have weak conflict?

We've been exploring how conflict and tension are important to a story, so why are they so often missing from our books? I have several friends who are agents or editors in the business, and I've never heard them complain of "too much tension" in the submissions they see. Why, if we know conflict and tension are important, do we fail to put them in our manuscripts?

We love our characters

As writers, we spend a lot of time with our characters. They take up real estate in our brains. They follow us around while we live our lives, reminding us what they're going through and suggesting what they might do next. Somewhere along the way, you'll find yourself caring about them. Heck, you might even love them. Even a writer with a cold, dark heart is sometimes swayed to fall in love with their imaginary friends. And caring about them can make it hard to crush their hopes and dreams. (That is, if you're a decent person.)

It can be hard to hurt people—even imaginary people—if we like them. There is a temptation to go easy on them, to let them off the hook at the last minute. Ignore this feeling. Draw on your inner serial killer. Remember that the more you throw at them, and the more they struggle, the greater the payoff will be in the end. Also, remember they are imaginary. No actual people are harmed in the making of your story.

We give up too easily

There are times when we're plotting what happens next in our story, and we go with our first idea before moving quickly on to the next plot point. We've failed to ask ourselves, "Did I make this as bad as possible? Did I squeeze every bit of conflict out of a scene and the characters, or did I settle for the first answer?"

Donald Maass, in his books and workshops, encourages writers to brainstorm a list of possible things that could happen next. He then points out that the best ideas often appear much lower on the list. The element of surprise, for example, isn't always a matter of something jumping out of nowhere; it can mean the character behaving in a way that we didn't expect.

Some readers (the kind we like most of all) are avid readers. They don't read a book every so often. They *consume* books. When they wander past bookstores, they are sucked in by its inescapable gravitational beam. As a result, they are *savvy* readers. They can often predict what a character will do and what will happen next in the story. When you surprise them by making a character react, or a scene unfold, in an unexpected way, they will sit up and take notice. When you are problem solving how to get a character out of a situation and you take the first solution that comes to you, keep in mind that your first choice is most likely what will first occur to the reader as well.

We worry it's too much

I've heard some writers express concern that they don't want to have *too* many bad things befall their characters because they worry that it will seem unrealistic. But fiction isn't real life. Consider Scarlett O'Hara. Not only did the man she love marry someone else, but she also dealt with war, marriage to a man she didn't love, unplanned pregnancy, the death of her first husband, marriage to her sister's fiancé, her mom's death, her dad's death, her second husband's death, marriage again (this time to a scoundrel), her daughter's birth, her daughter's death, a miscarriage, the incineration of her town, childbirth in the middle of a war, and the realization that she really loves the scoundrel—only for him to say he doesn't love her anymore.

And that's just the bigger conflicts. She's also dealing with friends and family, starting her own business and trying to figure out what to wear to important events.

You don't need to include this level of conflict in your stories (although, why the heck not?), but if you are feeling like it might be too much, consider Scarlett. She'd handle whatever you threw at her before lunch and still have time left in her day to make a dress out of curtains.

Readers delight in seeing characters get themselves out of complicated situations. The more complex the situation, the larger the problems, the more serious the conflict, the more reason we have to cheer when the character is ultimately successful. It is likely far easier to scale some of your conflict back than it is to add it in.

The good news is that conflict can be layered. When a character has a problem, they take an action to make things better. And that action can cause *new* problems. For example, a character that doesn't want to go to a work party might lie about having a conflicting event. But that lie leads people to make assumptions, compelling the character to tell new and more detailed lies… and you can see things begin to spiral out of control.

We're scared

Another reason you may be avoiding conflict is that you don't know how to resolve it in your story. You may be afraid that you'll paint yourself into a corner with no way to get out. The more difficult you make it for your character, the more difficult you make it for yourself as a writer. You're not the first (or last) writer to doubt your abilities in this area.

It may well be easier to let our characters—and ourselves —off the hook than to push ourselves. But have faith in yourself as a writer. It may take a while, and there may be some banging of your head on the desk, but you will rise to the challenge.

The book *Scrappy Rough Draft by Donna Barker* looks at the things that get in the way of our desire to get words on the page. She draws on research and science to provide coping strategies. Fear is something that most writers struggle with at some point, be it in a first scrappy draft or the tenth revision of a book. We want to do the stories in our head justice. We want readers to love the story as much as we do. We want the story to be the best it can be, and we may be second-guessing ourselves.

If you're struggling with how to resolve challenges the character faces, brainstorm with other writers. Go big. Let your ideas run wild. Remind yourself that you got this— you're a badass storyteller who can write your way out of anything. Remember, if you have to, you can always ease back on the conflict. It's always easier to dial back in revision than it is to dial up.

Your Turn

- Be honest. Have you gone too easy on your characters with conflict in your manuscript?
- What is the reason you've backed down on pushing the conflict? What is it about conflict that scares you or makes you uncomfortable?
- Create a list of every possible thing that could go

<u>wrong for your characters</u>, and don't hold back. Keep thinking of options until you're down to ideas that seem absurd—and then make yourself list at least two more. Sit on those ideas for a couple of days, and then revisit the list. Are there things you can add to your manuscript?

- Reach out to another writer and offer to provide them with conflict ideas for their manuscript if they'll provide ideas for your story. Having someone to chat with about book ideas can be a great support when you need to get outside your head to discover what's working and what isn't.

UNDERSTANDING CONFLICT RESPONSE

We're going to talk in detail about different ways your characters may respond to conflict, but it may be helpful first to understand how our animal brain responds. Our brains are the result of evolution, and a part of evolution is the overwhelming desire for survival. Our brains are hardwired to constantly evaluate needs (wants) and threats (conflicts) in order to ensure survival.

A number of things happen to your brain chemistry to help you respond to these types of conflicts or threats. (Don't worry, there isn't going to be a test!) One of these is the chemical production of cortisol. Think of cortisol as an early warning system for your brain. It assists your body's response. For example, it may slow your digestive system if it perceives your need to flee. You don't want part of your body focused on getting rid of that burger if you're about to become a bear snack. You want all systems focused on the priority, so raising your heart rate becomes more important in the moment than processing food.

But your brain doesn't know the difference between emotional pain and physical pain. That is, it can't tell the difference between a stalking lion and a guy determined to break your heart. It will respond the same way. Years of evolution, so many great design features—and yet that brain still has some big flaws. This means you may end up with an excess of cortisol in your body as your brain tries to deal with a range of stressful and painful events. And the problem is that while outrunning a lion attack only takes so much time, emotional challenges—like that relationship filled with heartache—can go on for months or years with no respite. That's a lot of cortisol flowing around. Too much cortisol in your system results in things like depression, anxiety, weight gain, heart disease and trouble sleeping.

When the brain is faced with a threat or conflict, science tells us it will respond in one of four ways: fight, flight, freezing or fawning. (If you're interested in understanding how your brain chemistry can be changed to cope with negativity, check out *The Science of Positivity* by Loretta Graziano Breuning, which goes into much more detail.)

Our brain is, at the most basic level, hard-wired with these four basic responses to pain or danger. These responses often happen at an instinctive level before we even pause to think. When planning how your character will react in a conflict situation, understand that first, your brain will want to go in one of the following four directions. If the conflict isn't immediate—if it isn't that pesky bear running straight toward you—your reason may override the chemical response. But it is still happening.

Let's take a look at the four responses.

Fight

In this response the brain tells you, *"Uh-oh, trouble. Get 'em!"* The brain will weigh this choice very carefully because fighting comes with inherent risks, including injury. Your evolutionary brain may not be complicated, but it's smart enough to know that being injured in the wild comes with a high cost. If you can't keep up with the pack, you risk being picked off, abandoned or eaten by your pack mates. (Mother Nature can be a real bitch.) As a result, your brain evaluates if the fight response is likely to turn out well before it decides to start swinging. If the conflict is a lion and you're a bunny, even your simple mammal brain is thinking that this isn't a great match-up. There's a reason nature shows don't feature a lot of scenes where bunnies are attacking lions.

If your conflict response is to fight, it's because you believe you have the ability to win or you feel you have no other choices. Even the bunny may come out swinging if it feels it has no other alternative.

Your Turn

- Does your story include circumstances in which your character has to fight for survival?

- Is their decision to fight a good one? Or do they not understand they're likely to lose?
- What would push your character to finally take a swing at someone?

Flee

This response to conflict may not seem very brave or noble, but it's a very legitimate choice. Fleeing, in fact, is the most common mammal response to threat. If you can get away without putting yourself at risk, that's the option you'll take. In the wild, even a minor injury can put you at risk of being targeted by a predator or vulnerable to infection and death. Your brain is hard-wired to think, "Fighting another day seems reasonable. Let's skedaddle." (For the record, I have long wanted to use skedaddle in a sentence.)

So why wouldn't someone flee all the time? Again, it comes down to a question of survival. If I'm starving, I may not run away when confronted with someone else who wants my dinner. I will take a stand because my life depends on winning. However, if I know I will live to fight another day, fleeing may seem like a better option.

Fleeing is a form of conflict avoidance. In the section below, I'll discuss the various reasons why a character might avoid conflict, but note that they are all ways of avoiding a pain (injury) response—even if that injury is emotional instead of physical. After all, our dumb brains don't understand that there's a difference.

Your Turn

- If your character runs from a conflict, how do they feel about that decision? Are they disappointed in themselves?
- How do the people around them view that decision?
- What "injury" (physical, but more likely emotional) do they risk if they fight? What do they risk if they don't take a stand at this point?
- Is your character the lion or the bunny in this fight?

Freeze

You've likely heard the term "a deer in the headlights." It references an animal's natural tendency at times to freeze in the face of conflict. This doesn't work very well for the deer facing down a car, but it does work occasionally with other predators. If an animal determines that it can't fight or flee, it may give freezing a chance. Its heartbeat and breath will slow, and it will hold still in an attempt to convince the predator that "there's nothing to see here. Move along."

If you love the *Jurassic Park* movies, you know that should you ever encounter a T-Rex (granted, a low level of risk) you're more likely to survive if you freeze. Those who run end up as T-Rex snacks because people rarely win speed races against T-Rexes. And while we may not face a lot of killer dinosaurs in our lifetimes, there are other instances where freezing may work. I live in a part of the world where we get bears. Each spring the city sends out a nice "bear aware" flyer full of helpful hints including how to lock up your garbage and if you should confront a bear to avoid running away. The flyer points out helpfully that "a bear may chase you because prey runs." Translation? Stand still.

Let's take bears and dinos out of the situation. Imagine your boss is on a rampage, wanting someone's head because something in the office went very wrong. People will freeze in their cubicles, not even looking up as he lumbers past, because they want to avoid being the focus of his attention. For the same reason, children may freeze in place when they hear an angry parent in the other room.

Your Turn

- What or who is the T-Rex in your character's life—the one they freeze to avoid?
- How do they feel when they freeze?
- Would your character speak up or stay frozen if they saw someone else attacked?

Fawn

The final way mammals respond to threat is with submission or fawning. Many mammal groups (wolves, apes, etc.) maintain a strict hierarchy, and those who live within the group know their place. When faced with someone who is dominant, the less dominant creature will show signs of submission: not looking the other in the eye, slumping, or—my dog's favourite option—rolling over and exposing his belly. (After all, you never know when a sign of submission might lead to a good belly rub!) The submissive person knows that facing the dominant person head-on will likely lead to aggression and trouble, so it's far better to communicate your understanding that they are the alpha dog.

Ever see someone who responds to a bully by being even nicer to them? They will do nice things for the bully in an effort to avoid being the target of that person's wrath. They may even be nicer to the bully than they are to people who are kind to them. Have you ever praised your boss and his *brilliant* idea—technically your brilliant idea, but hey, who cares—because you know there is no point in arguing with him? You're fawning.

If a character is married to a controlling personality who they feel they have to "manage," they may fawn over them if they sense their spouse is in a mood. They rush to make a cocktail, rub their shoulders, and don't say a peep when their spouse turns off *Downton Abbey* in order to watch Sunday night football. They are exposing their belly. They are hoping to avoid a conflict by acknowledging that the other person is dominant.

Your Turn

- Does your character ever use fawning as a response to conflict?
- How do they feel about themselves if they do this?
- Does anyone fawn over them? How do they respond?

7

CONFLICT AND CHARACTERS

We've looked at conflict from the writer's perspective and explored the animal's instinctive response. Now let's talk about it from a character's perspective. To do this, let's look at how non-imaginary (some might call them real) people deal with conflict.

If you've read my book *Build Better Characters*, you know I have a counselling background. I frequently turn to the training I did as a counsellor to help me understand how to craft realistic characters on the page. Psychologists have done a lot of research on all aspects of human behaviour to understand how and why people act and react the way that they do. In this book, I draw on the same experience to show you how people respond to conflict.

In *Build Better Characters*, I point out that a great resource for writers is the self-help section of the bookstore or library. No matter what situation or conflict your character is dealing with, I guarantee there are books detailing how to cope with it. Check them out to get ideas and deepen your understanding of how people might respond in those scenarios.

Conflict avoidance

The truth is that avoidance is the most common response to conflict. It makes sense that most people don't want to be involved with situations (or individuals) that result in tension and friction. As noted above about the animal kingdom, fleeing is often the safest response. Why risk injury when you can back away? But there are specific reasons, beyond the instinctive, why people avoid conflict. Here are a few.

Family dynamics

If you come from a family that avoids conflict, you're likely to do it as well. Consider your character's family dynamics around conflict. What skills did they learn about dealing with conflict? We learn these responses early in life and tend to replicate them in future relationships. Some families have fights or blow-ups over a range of topics, while other families rarely even raise their voices. (This doesn't mean there isn't a seething resentment.)

Past experience

Ever heard the cliché "once bitten, twice shy"? It means that if you've had a bad experience, you're unlikely to want to repeat it. This is why most of us don't go around touching hot stoves more than once. If people have had a bad experience with conflict in the past, they may be reluctant to tackle it again.

Consider your character's past interactions. If they've had a lot of conflict with someone in the past, they may go out of their way to avoid it with that person, or even other people, in the future.

Feeling not heard

The purpose of healthy conflict is to discuss issues and negotiate a way forward. If you feel that you're in conflict with people who don't listen to your views, who speak over you, or who ignore your perspective, you may choose to avoid future interactions. After all, if there's no chance it's going to fix things, why bother? There are few things more frustrating than having an opinion you want to share pushed aside. Dominant people can take over arguments and steamroll quieter individuals. If your character is quieter, they may feel it's not worthwhile to keep trying.

Lack of confidence

Ah, self-confidence. It really does come in handy in life. This could be why there are so many books and podcasts on how to develop it. If you lack confidence in yourself, you're likely reluctant to view your opinions as important or valid compared to the opinions of others. If someone disagrees with a character who lacks self-confidence, the insecure character may avoid discussions because they automatically assume the other person must be right. Even when they know they are right, they may still back down because they think, *who would want to listen to me anyway?*

People pleasing or avoiding hurt

Is your character highly empathic? It's possible they will avoid conflict because they don't want to hurt someone else by disagreeing with them. There's also a fine line between caring for others out of true empathy and being a people pleaser—putting one's own needs behind others if it means making others happy. How much does your character value other people's happiness? Will they put it ahead of their own self-interest? It's important to note that the other person may not even be hurt or upset by the possible conflict. What matters is that the person avoids conflict because they *perceive* that the other person may be upset. Above, I discussed family dynamics and history. This may be one area in which an individual's past experience influences how they behave with others.

Unclear perspective

Conflict happens as a result of differing opinions. But this means you have to have one! Have you ever been asked your opinion and suddenly realized that you aren't sure? Perhaps you haven't considered it before, or you feel you need more information. If you aren't sure where you stand on an issue, you will likely be reluctant to take a stand in an argument.

Does your character feel a desire to know all sides of an issue before they stake out their perspective? Perhaps they are trying to determine what core values are involved in, or impacted by, a particular perspective.

Fear of loss

Conflict has differing levels of impact. A couple that is arguing about whether to go for Italian or sushi for dinner may not worry that their relationship is at stake. (I suppose it depends how strongly you feel about pasta—pretty strongly, in my case.) However, if a couple is in conflict over having children or remaining child free, they could break up over it. Avoiding the conflict likely doesn't help much in the long term, but in the short term it may mean putting off a very painful end to a relationship.

Another example of how fear of loss motivates conflict avoidance is an individual who fears that they aren't performing the way their boss expects. They may put off discussing the issue with their employer because they're afraid it will bring everything to a head and they'll be fired. If what they could lose as a result of the fight is too valuable to put at risk, they may avoid the fight altogether.

Not one thing more

Is your character exhausted? Have they been swimming upstream for a long period of time, struggling to take on their personal life, family, friends, work and home? When that happens, some individuals may decide that it simply isn't worth it to have another argument. They may feel that they don't have the resources or reserve energy to deal with another issue or fight. About anything. They may give in, even if, in another time or place, the issue would matter to them.

People do have limits. If someone gets pushed to those limits over a long period of time, they can reach a point where they no longer care. Or, to put it crudely, they have no more fu$*s to give. Your character may walk away from conflict to avoid adding anything else to their already-full plate.

Your Turn

- How does your character's family deal with conflict? Are they comfortable with that response?
- If you have two characters in a relationship, consider having them come from families with very different responses to conflict. How will they negotiate what conflict looks like in their relationship?
- What is your character's past experience with conflict? Did it go well?
- Does your character feel their perspective is being heard? Are they hearing others?
- How would your protagonist hurt another character they care about by raising conflict?
- On a scale from one to ten, where one means they have very clear personal boundaries and ten means they are a doormat, how much of a people pleaser is your character?
- How clearly does your character know where they stand on an issue? Are there things they still need to figure out?
- What conflict might your character put off because of a fear of loss? What would they potentially lose if a fight were to happen?
- What does your character already have on their plate? Are they too exhausted for another argument? Is there something they would normally care a lot about that they currently don't have the energy to cope with?

When conflict avoidance blows up

In some cases, avoidance works really well. Perhaps the argument isn't that important, or the individual can let go of things in the past and move forward with no hard feelings.

But perhaps not.

If an individual avoids conflict and stores up frustration until they finally blow, it doesn't usually end well. The psychological term for avoiding things until they explode is "gunnysacking." This refers to the idea of saving up annoyances and problems and tucking them away (in a sack) rather than dealing with them. Eventually all these pent-up issues and grievances blow and escape the sack. It's one thing to avoid problems, and it's another to avoid them but still hang on to them. It's not healthy in real life, but in fiction, the moment when that sack finally blows and all those resentments come flying out can be interesting to see. Keep in mind some people have a pretty large gunnysack. They can hang onto a lot of things before they explode. Other people have a thin, sandwich-baggie-sized gunnysack. They could lose everything in record time.

Your Turn

○ Does your character avoid problems but still hang on to their annoyance?

- What past experiences are already in their bag? How large is their bag?
- What will be the issue that makes this finally blow?

The opposite of conflict avoidance

Your character may be avoiding conflict for a range of reasons, but what about characters who seem to thrive on it? There are people out there who, when they see a potential conflict, run toward it at full speed with a giant Viking, 'Whoop.' It can be helpful to understand why these individuals may choose conflict.

The opportunity to be right

There are few issues for which there is a clear right or wrong side (one exception being that chocolate is the best thing to ever happen to humanity). However, there are individuals who feel that there *is* often a right and wrong way. And typically, what they view to be right just happens to be the correct answer for everyone. What a coincidence! Now if they could only get everyone to agree, the world would run much more smoothly.

Individuals with this perspective struggle if someone disagrees with them, because it feels like a personal attack. To them, the person disagreeing is not simply stating a different opinion but is saying that their perspective is *wrong*. And that is not okay. As a result, they're more likely to dig in and argue because to negotiate or give in means giving up their own opinion.

Consider the hot-button issue of politics in our polarized society. Regardless of where you stand on the political spectrum, there are always people on the other side. It could even be argued that having a range of opinions has made our societies stronger. However, as politics have become more personal, someone with an alternate perspective can be made to feel that they are the enemy. It's become common to default to name calling and disparaging other people for their views.

Your Turn

- Does your character believe they are right in almost all situations? How do they cope with people who disagree?
- Are there specific issues that feel personal to your character? Issues over which they believe anyone who opposes them doesn't simply have another opinion, but is actively wrong?

Overgeneralization

Ever had a person imply that because you feel a certain way about issue A, you must also feel that way about issues B, C, D and E? It is easy to generalize, and if you do, it tends to create trickier conflict because a lot more is at stake than you initially anticipated when the discussion began.

For example, if my spouse accuses me of failing to clean up the dishes after dinner, a few issues will arise. While there's the issue of if I did or didn't wash them, this argument can quickly turn into "you never pull your weight around the house." And once you throw down a "never" or "always," you've used some fighting words. I will argue much harder and level up the argument because no way will I agree that I never help out or don't do my fair share. Why, just last week I made dinner every night! When situations become overgeneralized, it will increase conflict.

Or, since we spoke about politics earlier, if someone says, "If you vote for this person this means that you also believe X and Y," you may become angry because you feel you're being accused of something unfairly or inaccurately.

Your Turn

- Have you ever been in an argument about one issue, and the other individual overgeneralized it to include several things that you didn't agree with? How did you respond?
- How can you expand one of your character's conflicts to include more than the issue at hand?

Defence can be the best offence

Some individuals may increase conflict in a backward way. They will become extremely defensive if accused of anything. They won't take any responsibility or recognize that they have contributed to a conflict. This behaviour leaves the other individual holding all the blame. They won't like that. They will be much more likely to push back and thus worsen the conflict.

Your Turn

- Does your character take responsibility for the things they've done, or do they always deny wrongdoing?
- Is there an argument in your manuscript where another character can avoid taking responsibility, leaving your protagonist holding the bag?

Desire for drama

There are people who like conflict because it makes them feel alive. Sparkly! Conflict is exciting. When things are too peaceful, too content, they feel bored. They will pick arguments or engage in conflict because it gives them a focus. They enjoy the high that comes from conflict—the rush of brain chemicals and the feeling of engagement. As an official fan of the no-drama-llama approach to life, this drives me crazy, but there are many people who thrive on high drama. And if it doesn't happen naturally, they'll go out of their way to create it.

Have you ever known a couple (or been in a relationship) that seems to court conflict—just so that when the conflict is over, they will make up? People in these relationships feel more loved because the other person cares enough to have the argument. High emotions can be sexy.

Another example of a person who desires drama is a friend who swings from one disaster to another. She's either in a fight with a family member—and they are *never speaking to each other again*—or she and her spouse are on the verge of breakup, or her job is falling apart. And that's just on a Tuesday.

Shelby

Your Turn

- Does your character have a flair for the dramatic? Do they enjoy conflict because it makes them feel alive?
- Is there someone in your character's life who thrives on drama? How do they react to conflict?
- If your character has a relationship that thrives on conflict, what do they enjoy about it?

High-conflict personality

We've talked about some things that may increase conflict, but there is another area that is worth mentioning. There is a psychological term called High-Conflict Personality (HCP). This is often categorized as a personality disorder. Individuals with this condition may have personality traits that include being dramatic, emotional or erratic. These constitute long-standing personality issues in their life that often negatively impact their ability to interact with others (both at work and at home). When we're talking about HCP, we're talking about extreme levels of these behaviours.

Psychology isn't clear about what causes HCP, but like many deep-rooted, maladaptive behaviours, there does seem to be a connection to abuse or neglect early in life. Keep in mind screenwriting coach Michael Hauge's term, "the hole in the soul." Hauge advises writers that most of us have a "hole" that emerges as a result of some experience we've had, usually in early childhood. Because of that hole, we engage in patterns of behaviour to try to either fill that hole or paper over it, so no one else knows it's there. High-Conflict Personality is an extreme example of that behaviour, but it does exist.

If you have a character who thrives on conflict, consider their backstory. What happened to them to result in their behaviour? (Exercises on determining backstory can be found in *Build Better Characters*.)

What traits do people with HCP share?

- They are instigators of conflict. Remember the kid who would poke you with a pencil in kindergarten until you finally snapped? Then he would sit back and enjoy watching you get all riled up. That is someone who enjoys conflict because they get a "reward" when others respond. You see this *constantly* online. These individuals don't even seem to have particularly strong opinions—what they enjoy is the battle. They will go online and say inflammatory things until someone finally snaps.

- They're always in the middle of conflict. Someone with this personality is always in the thick of things. Because they enjoy conflict, they will stick themselves in the middle whenever they can— even if the argument isn't theirs.

- They see conflict as a defining part of relationships. While we know that conflict is a normal and important part of healthy relationships, someone with HCP sees conflict as integral to any relationship. If there isn't conflict, they will seek it out and find a way to raise issues.

- They are skilled escalators of conflict. Conflict typically grows. Most people don't often go from zero to sixty; they build up to it. We'll discuss later in the book how conflict can escalate, but people with this personality are skilled at pushing others along until a small conflict becomes much larger.

- They deflect responsibility. We've already discussed how people with this personality type tend to seek out conflict and, when they find it, bang the drum to make it even larger. If negative consequences result, these individuals are really skilled at looking around and blaming others for that conflict. It wasn't them! It was how other people responded that cause the problem. Individuals with this personality will consistently blame others for the negative consequences of a conflict (such as being fired or losing a relationship) and will frame themselves as victims. They will resist seeing themselves as in any way responsible for the escalation of events.

- They display poor empathy. One of the strongest skills that a person can possess is the ability to see a situation from another's perspective. Even if you disagree with someone, attempting to understand their view will serve you well. Individuals with HCP struggle to understand views other than their own. They are certain that they are right and believe that anyone who opposes them is *wrong* and simply needs to accept that. When you hear terms like "you are with me or you're against me," it's a sign of someone who possesses at least some of this world view.

The challenge with HCP and many other personality disorders is that they can be very hard to treat. But characters who see the world in black and white or right and wrong can be a delight to write. They sow conflict wherever they go. While you should avoid these people in real life, fiction is a place to embrace them and the problems they will cause for both themselves and others.

Other unhealthy ways to respond to conflict

Never fear, there are many more ways to deal negatively with conflict than the primary ways I've discussed above. One thing you learn as a counsellor is that there are as many ways to be dysfunctional as there are people. (This is one of the many reasons there is so much job security in working as a counsellor.)

Lack of empathy

Some people find that exposure to conflict can lead to a lack of empathy. This is commonly seen in individuals who have to deal with difficult, high-stress, or high-conflict situations on a regular basis. A relative of mine works for her local police department. Her job may be to serve and protect, but it also means she spends a significant amount of time interacting with individuals who are not at their best. She's been spit on, yelled at, had shots fired in her direction, and often reaches into pockets only to find needles.

It's safe to say that she witnesses or experiences conflict on a near-daily basis. One way that this has impacted her is that she has a reduced level of empathy, in particular for strangers. She's cynical about other people's reactions and has low expectations of strangers.

I've also seen this in people who work in high-emotion settings such as hospitals. I worked for years in a rehabilitation hospital, where our clients were all dealing with some kind of traumatic injury. My co-workers and I found different ways to cope with this high emotion on a daily basis. Dark humour is a common response, as is learning to compartmentalize so that you can focus.

Withdrawal of emotion

Have you ever been the recipient of the silent treatment? That awkward moment of sitting at a table while someone turns to another person and says, "Will you ask Eileen to pass the salt?" while refusing to make eye contact with you? Nothing will bring you back to junior-high PTSD quite like the silent treatment (and that really bad haircut your mom made you get.)

Often the withdrawal of emotion is worse than a blow-up. This is why some individuals in a conflict will push others into showing *any* kind of response. The person withdrawing may be doing it because they no longer feel they can deal with the strong emotions they're experiencing or the up and down that comes with conflict. Their way to deal with that stress and friction is to remove themselves emotionally.

Another reason for withdrawal is to punish the other person. Rather than engage in the conflict, the individual will withhold their emotion. Feeling emotionally connected to others taps into our evolutionary desire to be a part of a pack. If someone in our circle threatens to withdraw a connection, we'll feel threatened. This can cause the other individuals in the relationship to fear difficult situations because they may result in a loss of emotional contact. As a result, the person won't raise issues that may need to be talked about.

Passive aggression

This conflict-management strategy may be the most fun to put into your manuscript as it can show up in so many ways. Passive aggression is like aggression's annoying cousin. It's like trying to nail down Jell-O. It's there, but pinpointing it directly can be a challenge. This allows the other person to slide away from blame or conflict.

Maybe you're "accidentally" left off an email to a group of friends planning an event. Or someone fails to mention they forgot something and they need to go back home to get it, until you've already left for an event. *Oopsie, guess we'll be late to that thing that's really important to you.*

The secret to passive aggression is <u>deniability</u>. If you call out a person who is passive aggressive, they will widen their eyes, point tentatively to their chest and say, "Who me?" This can also make the person who raised the issue feel that perhaps it's all in their head. They're left wondering if they've been gaslit.

A common passive-aggressive tactic is <u>subtle sabotage</u>. This can take form of a boss who doesn't give you all the information for a project you were assigned, so that when you do learn all the information, you have to start again. Or it can take the form of a "helpful" spouse who drops your best outfit off at the dry cleaner the night before you fly out for a business trip that they didn't want you to go on. *Sorry. Guess you'll have to wear something else. I was just trying to be helpful.*

Consider the <u>passive-aggressive superpower of the non-compliment compliment</u>. "Great outfit. So many people would be afraid to wear something so busy." My former mother-in-law (whom I actually really love, but who could deliver passive aggression like a boss) once told me, "You keep a lovely home for a woman who works." I stewed on that for months—and apparently I'm still working through it.

The non-compliment compliment is a very close relative to the <u>disguised insult</u>. Examples of this include "I don't want to upset you, but [insert something that can only be upsetting, but that you now feel you can't be upset about]." The belief that you can absolve yourself of rudeness by saying "I told you ahead of time" is classic passive aggression. *I don't mean to be rude, but your dinner turned out really badly. I could hardly choke it down.* As Dr. Phil would tell you, the word *but* tends to negate whatever came before it. I feel really bad, *but*... I don't mean to upset you, *but*... I was going to do that, *but*...

"I'm not racist/ sexist/ homophobic, but..."

How a character deals with a passive aggressive person depends on the story they tell themselves about what they are experiencing. For example, a person with weaker self-esteem due to a turbulent childhood may tell themselves that what happened was their fault. A character with anger issues may blow up. Yet another may have a high degree of confidence and insight and recognize that the passive aggressive person's issue is *their* problem.

Your Turn

- Does your character have empathy burnout? What led to this? Write a journal entry about a time in the past when they faced a similar situation but had *all the feels*.   *Kyra*
- Does your character ever withhold emotion? What do they tell themselves about why they are doing this?
- If your character is in conflict with someone who withdraws emotion, how does this make them feel? Do they then give in?

- Would you describe any of your characters as passive aggressive? If your character is passive aggressive, do they know it, or do they think they're behaving innocently? How does this passive aggression show up in their interactions?
- If your character interacts with someone who is passive aggressive, how do they respond?

Healthy ways to manage conflict

You're putting your character under a lot of stress in the book as they navigate various internal and external conflicts. We've been discussing unhealthy ways that your character may respond, but they may also have healthy responses to conflict.

My book *Build Better Characters* discusses Emotional Intelligence (EQi) in detail. It provides a framework to consider how personality impacts different aspects of a character's reactions. An individual with a good emotional intelligence has strengths and skills that are very helpful when navigating a high-stress situation. You can download the free EQi resources that accompany the book from:

http://creativeacademyforwriters.com/ resources/buildbettercharacters/

There are a few aspects of emotional intelligence that make a significant difference to the outcome of conflicts. These include:

- an understanding of what's really troubling other people and an ability to demonstrate empathy;
- an understanding of one's own emotions—and what led to those emotions;
- the ability to communicate clearly and effectively with others;
- an awareness that one's own perception of a situation may be subjective and coloured by personal perspectives (in emotional intelligence terms, this is called reality testing); and
- a high level of stress tolerance and an ability to remain calm and evaluate options even when the situation is challenging.

Conflict Resolution

I've spent a lot of time discussing how to increase conflict, but it's important to note that seeing a character resolve a conflict in a healthy way or acknowledge the unhelpfulness of their actions can be a great emotional break for the reader. We like individuals who learn from mistakes. Granted, it may take your character a while to sort out what they're doing wrong, but don't feel that they can never have a healthy response.

Your Turn

- Review the fifteen different aspects of emotional intelligence as listed on the resources page in the Creative Academy for Writers http://creativeacademyforwriters.com/resources/

buildbettercharacters/ and identify if your character has specific strengths in any of these areas. How does this help them in conflict situations?

- Does your character have any specific weaknesses in emotional intelligence? How does that impact their ability to cope with conflict?

WHAT CAUSES CONFLICT?

Given that so many of us don't like conflict, why does it happen? If we can all agree that all the world needs is love, why do we so often end up in an argument instead?

Hopefully, I've convinced you that your manuscript needs conflict, but you may be wondering how to raise conflict so that it feels organic instead of dropped in.

Here are some primary issues that lead to conflict between individuals.

Differing needs or wants

Imagine we're on vacation together, and we have only one day in Paris. You want to see the Eiffel Tower, and I want to go to the *Musée de la Préfecture de Police,* a true crime museum. If we don't have time to do both, one of us is going to be upset. (I would point out here that you can see the Eiffel Tower on TV. I could buy you a poster of it. We're talking a cool, once-in-a-lifetime experience with the crime museum, but hey, whatever. If you want to be predictable, so be it.) Whenever two people want different things, the potential for conflict exists. And if it is about something one person *needs*, the amount of that conflict is going to go up.

This conflict about differing needs and wants also exists inside of each of us. Do you ever *need* to get into a regular habit at the gym, but you also *want* to sleep for thirty more minutes to avoid killing your co-workers or falling asleep in the budget meeting later in the day?

Perhaps you *want* security, but you also *need* to spread your wings and take on new risks to reach your dreams. Hypothetically—just imagine this for a moment with me— you don't like when people reject you. You don't like to hear that something you created isn't as good as you thought it was. You have a good life. You don't need a bunch of people telling you that they don't like the things you're passionate about.

But you also want to write a book.

Uh-oh.

And if you want your book in the hands of readers, if you need to tell your story, it means you are going to have to let go of that safety and security, and that's hard. It means risking all those things you don't want to happen. Once you write a book, you're going to deal with rejection. It might be agents or editors, or it might be readers who reject what you have to say. That's friction. That's conflict.

Your Turn

- What does your character want in the story? Is it possible for them to also want the opposite?
- Consider characters in your manuscript. Can you put their wants and needs in opposition?

Differing values

Values are fundamental beliefs that drive our actions. They tend to run deep and be very important to us. They're how we structure our sense of right and wrong in the world. Examples of values include the belief that honesty is essential, that family is the most important, that loyalty is required between friends, and that trust must be earned. I talked in Chapter Three about internal value conflicts, but we should take a look at how values impact others.

The challenge is that not everyone shares our values. (I know! How annoying is that?) When people act outside our core values, conflict will ensue. Review the core values you identified for your character in Chapter Three. In that section, the focus was on conflict with our own values, but this time, consider how your values interact with others.

Remember how I talked about the value I place on being on time? As you might recall, I'm the one parked a block away from your place before a dinner party because though I may not have the best social skills, even I know showing up thirty minutes early is not okay. However, I have a friend who follows what we refer to as "island time." This refers to her belief that timelines and meeting times are more of a guideline or a suggestion. This has caused friction in our relationship. I project my value judgement about punctuality onto her. I believe that being on time means you respect the other person; therefore, someone who isn't on time to meet me must not see our relationship as important.

Except it doesn't mean that to her. To her, being late is no big deal.

For our relationship to work, we both had to shift our values. She had to understand that punctuality meant a lot to me, and that if she couldn't be on time, at least she should aim to be close. I had to learn that she has millions of wonderful qualities but that being on time isn't one of them. That her tendency to be late is no reflection of how she feels about me. Thus, I always bring a book when we're getting together.

Some people survive value differences by negotiating, as my friend and I did. Some people shift their values in order to match with the other person. Others never get over it, and it becomes a constant source of conflict. You may know people who value organization but are married to people who apparently prefer to live in chaos, where you can't find anything and the dust bunnies have grown to the size of Volkswagens. (Not that I would make any sort of value judgement on which is better. Heavens, no.) Do they work it out? Do they find a happy medium, or does the organized person clean up after their spouse and resent it the whole time?

Different ideas or perspectives

People have different ideas about politics, climate change, how to best deal with a crying child, the impact of various historical events, how to handle a problem at the office, you name it. Those perspectives may be driven by core values, experience, education or simply a gut feeling. How strongly you perceive your idea to be better, or "correct," compared to the other ideas on offer will impact how far you'll go to defend it.

Your Turn

Review the issues in your book. What is your character's perspective or opinion on these issues? Can you set up another character to oppose this?

Perception of threat

In all of the situations above, there's a common denominator—the perception of threat. Your characters may not be discussing a conflict that entails life-or-death stakes. (Although your character may be debating the best way to defuse that bomb, and that is pretty life-or-death.) However, even a simple conflict can feel life-or-death to you character depending on what they perceive they will lose if they lose the conflict.

For example, I may be in a conflict with a co-worker over who gets the new office chair. In theory, we're simply debating who needs (or deserves) the better chair. However, if I feel that my social standing at the office has been slipping, I may worry that if I back down about the chair, I will also give up my right to move into a more important work role. Then I will fight much harder than office furniture deserves. I'll talk about stakes later in this book, but for the moment, let's focus on perception.

Perception is often more important than reality. The lens through which we view reality is what drives our actions and interactions with others. We all have stories that we tell ourselves about the world and our place within it, and these stories are built up over time and through experiences.

Understanding perception—Rational Emotive Therapy

When I was in my counselling program, we learned a variety of counselling approaches, from Freud to Jung and everything in between. One approach that always stuck in my mind was Albert Ellis's Rational Emotive Therapy. While many particulars have left my memory—why I can remember the lyrics to most 80s tunes but not where I put my sunglasses is a mystery of getting older—one aspect of RET has stuck with me, in part because it's always made so much sense to me.

Ellis put forward the idea of A, B, C. (I told you this would be easy to remember.)

A is the activating event;

B is the belief about that event; and

C is the consequence of that belief.

Let's look at a common example. You're in a writing group. You've attended for a while, but you've never shared your own work. You finally work up the guts. Everyone is quiet while you read. After you read you excuse yourself to go the bathroom. When you come back into the room, everyone is laughing. When they see you, they stop laughing. That is the activating event, the A.

In that moment, your brain will fill in the gaps in your knowledge to make sense of what has just happened. That is your belief, B. If you are insecure (not that I know any writers who are insecure), you may decide that everyone is laughing because they are making fun of you and what you just read. You feel your face flush, your brain releases a wave of cortisol (the brain chemical that leaves you feeling a need to fight or flee), and you may feel the desire to throw up, lash out in rage, or erupt in tears. Or, if you're one of the truly lucky people out there, you'll feel all these things at the same moment.

Because of that belief, you will react. Perhaps you manage to get through the rest of the meeting, but you never go again. Or maybe you blast them, scream, *"You're all a bunch of wannabe, judgmental hacks!"* toss their papers to the floor and storm from the room. Either way, you've set up a consequence, the C. If they weren't talking about you before, they likely are now. Or, if you never go back, it's possible you miss the chance to network and grow as a writer. Those are all consequences of your belief.

If you experience the same activating event, but your belief is that you simply missed the joke, you will react differently. You'll likely sit back down and continue talking to the others. The consequence will be completely different. If they were talking about you, they may feel bad and think you handled the situation with class. Or perhaps you did just miss the joke, someone fills you in, and you get a laugh out of the situation as well.

This ABC scenario is the set-up of many story conflicts. It may be present in a romantic comedy where a misunderstanding about what has been seen keeps a couple apart until the end of the story, when love wins out. *Ohh... That woman you were hugging at the New Year's Eve party was your* sister? *Oops.*

ABC is also used in mystery novels in which a character sees a clue, for instance, that leads them to believe another character is innocent (or perhaps guilty). Later, they discover that their belief about what they saw led them to a false conclusion.

Once you start looking for this ABC set-up, you'll see it present in stories with families, space battles, magical creatures and everything in between. The truth is that we are all unreliable narrators. It is very difficult for us to separate objective reality from our own perceptions.

We look for things that buttress our already existing beliefs and tend to overlook, ignore, or explain away things that challenge it. Politics is a great example of this. I come from a conservative family. My dad in particular considers me to be a flaming liberal. When we talk about politics (which we do on occasion to drive my mom crazy), we will have very different takes on the same objective bits of news.

If you are a positive person, you will look for—and see—examples of the goodness of people as you move through your day. If you're more cynical, you will go through the same day but pick up on the negative things. The events of the day are often the same; it's what our brain notices and records that makes the difference. As a result, two characters may have very different experiences of the same day.

Your Turn

- Identify an activating event in your story. What is your character's belief about that event?
- Is that belief accurate? How does that belief change the consequence?
- Brainstorm a list of possible beliefs your character could have about an activating event. Would any of these lead to a more interesting outcome than the one you currently have?

Stress

Stress is a normal part of life. That doesn't mean we like it. Stress is our body's reaction to difficult situations. It can show up in physical or emotional ways. Conflict causes stress for most of us. That stress response then further impacts how we deal with that conflict. It's one big circle of maladjustment!

As a counsellor, I know that stress can't be avoided. There's even a compelling argument that we need a certain level of stress in our lives in order to grow. However, some people deal with that stress better than others.

Your Turn

How does your character deal with stress? Do they:

- become agitated or restless?
- lash out at others?
- withdraw?
- become very analytical?
- become very emotional?
- How does that stress show up in their body? Do they:
- pick their nails?
- chew the ends of their hair?
- bite the inside their cheek?
- bounce in place?
- feel nauseated?
- get headaches?
- experience tension across the shoulders (or in another area)?

If you're struggling to figure out how to show that your character is stressed, consider the excellent resource *The Emotion Thesaurus: A Writer's Guide to Character Expression* by Angela Ackerman and Becca Puglisi.

Stress impacts an individual's ability to deal with conflict, which in turn can cause more conflict. (As a writer, this idea fills me with glee.) When you have a conflict scene in your manuscript, remember that the fun doesn't have to stop there. Characters' responses to that conflict will provide you with an opportunity to add even more conflict. Characters who are feeling stressed may respond by:

- being unable to pick up on the other person's non-verbal communication;
- hearing only part of what the other person is saying or misunderstanding what is said; or
- confusing their own feelings.

Your Turn

- If you were to rank your character's stress tolerance on a scale of one to ten—with one meaning they fall apart at the smallest pressure and ten meaning they are calm and collected even during an apocalypse—where does your character fall?
- Prior to the beginning of the book, what was the most stressful event your character ever had to deal with?
- Does your character's stress tolerance change during the book?
- How do the people around your character deal with stress?

NON-VERBAL COMMUNICATION, HUMOUR AND CONFLICT

Non-verbal Communication

One of the things I discuss in *Build Better Characters* is how using skills that counsellors employ can help with your characters. Counsellors learn early on that what isn't said is often as important—or more important—that what is said aloud. Studies done by Dr. Albert Mehrabian broke down communication patterns by looking at how the brain determined meaning. He found that the interpretation of a message is seven percent verbal, thirty-eight percent vocal (tone, volume) and fifty-five percent visual. This is a fancy way of saying that if you are relying on dialogue as your primary form of communication, you're missing out on a huge opportunity.

There are a range of reasons we don't always share what we are actually thinking. It's possible that it wouldn't be polite. Or we may be afraid of another person's reaction—

we don't want to reveal that we find someone really attractive, or that we think our boss's bright idea is actually quite dim.

It is also possible that we don't know exactly what we're feeling, but when we communicate, our bodies may give us away. When you tell someone that *of course* you love them and think that entering a long-distance relationship so they can take a promotion is a great idea—all while looking down at your hands and biting on your lower lip —you may be saying more than you think. You may *want* to be okay with this plan. Perhaps you're not even sure what it is about it that bothers you. But things are not "just fine."

Another reason we hold back what we really want to say is to test another person. We are curious to know if they can tell what's really on our mind. We want to feel heard and understood, but we often want people to do it without having to tell them. I have a friend who is annoyed every holiday because her spouse never seems to get her what she really wants as a gift. However, she doesn't want to tell him what she wants because it's not "romantic." When she opens the gift under the tree, she tries to communicate, without actually saying anything, that she's less than thrilled with the present.

Although this book is about writing advice, allow me to slip in a relationship tip. If you don't want a vacuum for your birthday and your spouse is the kind of person who thinks you might like a handy appliance, you need to shut that shit down from the get-go. Maybe your spouse comes from a very practical family. Maybe their mom loved a good kitchen gadget for the holidays. If you don't like that kind of present, speak up or forever grind your teeth as year after year you unwrap a stainless-steel food processor because you vaguely hinted that you'd love something shiny under the tree.

Let's consider a non-verbal example. A partner has been flirting with the server at a restaurant. You're annoyed. You've talked about this, for crying out loud. It's not that you think they have to not notice attractive people, but would it be too much for them to rein it in when you are sitting *right* there? You clench your teeth. You answer questions with one-word responses. You cross your arms over your chest. Your partner then says, "Is everything okay?"

You arch an eyebrow and stare across the table. "Everything's fine."

Clue alert: Everything is *not* fine. It's very, very, very not fine.

Those with good insight (and emotional intelligence) are able to read the emotion in that statement. Others will gloss right past it. Either way, understanding non-verbal communication is really helpful for writers when dealing with communication between characters. Using the example above you have a few options:

- If you are writing from the POV of the character who is angry about the flirting, you can show the internal thought. Show us what they feel instead of what they say, which is "fine." What are they hoping to gain by not directly saying what they mean? Perhaps they want to see if their loved one can pick it up without being told. *If he loved me, I wouldn't have to tell him what was wrong. He would just know. He's playing dumb on purpose!*

- If you are writing from the POV of the character doing the flirting, do they pick up on the non-verbal cues? If yes, what do they think the cues mean? Perhaps they recognize that all that arm crossing is directed at them. *Great, I've stepped in it now. She's going to be in a bad mood all night.* However, it's also possible that they misread the situation and think their partner is angry about something else entirely. *Jeez, she must have had a really bad day at work. She's in a horrible mood.* Then you have a choice to make—do you want the reader to suspect they have the wrong belief, or do you want them to be in agreement with the flirter, only to discover later that they had it wrong?

- If you're writing from the POV of the flirter, and he does not pick up on the non-verbal cues, does the reader notice it? Are they thinking as they flip the pages, "Oh, buddy, pay attention. You're going to be in real trouble."

- You are the writer. The outcome of this argument is in your control. How do the characters' responses to this non-verbal situation change what happens next?

Your Turn

- Look at a conflict scene in your manuscript. What

non-verbal communication is shown on the page? Do the characters recognize what *isn't* being said?

- Challenge yourself to write a conflict scene in which the characters cannot say what they are really angry about. How much can you communicate without any dialogue?

Humour and conflict resolution

I believe there are few things in life that can't be made better by a good sense of humour. The ability to laugh when things are challenging is a survival skill I've honed over the years, and it has gotten me through many difficult times. Occasionally, I even have an appropriate sense of humour, but certainly not all the time. The ability to lower the tension of a situation by laughing can prevent or resolve disagreements.

The benefits of humour include:

- more easily broaching a difficult or awkward topic,
- defusing another person's anger,
- reframing a situation to make it feel less dire and put things into perspective, and
- providing a way to cope emotionally with conflict.

Your character may use humour as a way to lighten the mood. This has the added benefit of giving the reader a break from heavier emotions. Not only do you get to include conflict in the story, but you also gain a beat of humour. Talk about a win-win. The fact that two characters can laugh during a challenge also demonstrates intimacy and closeness. The reader sees the two characters going through something difficult and finding a way to laugh. That humour brings them closer.

In his book, *Writing Screenplays that Sell*, Michael Hauge looks at what makes a character likeable. In addition to other things, he lists humour. People like people who are funny. (This is basically the only reason I have a social life, because I'm otherwise the most socially awkward person you will meet. It also helps that I'm generally kind and reasonably smart, but humour is my selling point.) So using humour in your conflict scenes gives readers another reason to like your character.

Now for the other edge of the humour sword.

To paraphrase that great philosopher from the *Spider-Man* movies, Uncle Ben, "with great humour comes great responsibility." There has been a lot of damage done by individuals who say something cruel and then toss out, "I'm just joking!" When I see this, I want to push that person down into a steaming pile of dog poo and declare, "Just joking!" to see how they like it.

Any kind of humour that belittles or mocks another person, especially someone who is vulnerable, will not reduce conflict. If anything, it's going to ramp it up. The person on the receiving end of the barb may not respond at the time, but trust me, they will file away that little nugget of resentment, and it will come back.

Above, the idea of using humour to bring up a difficult topic is listed as a benefit, but it can also be a negative. There are people who will make a joke as a way of raising an issue, but without really providing an opportunity for discussion or resolution. They use their humour to score a point and then hide behind their "joke" if anyone wants to retaliate. If anything, it puts the other person even more on the defensive because they're left to wonder if they're being too sensitive.

Another source of conflict comes when a character says something they thought would be funny, only to realize once it's out there that it was actually hurtful. They may not have intended it to be hurtful, or perhaps the person misunderstood what they said, but either way, something that was meant to be a joke is now anything but.

If you have a character who uses humour as a weapon, it allows you to play with expectations. The reader may not be sure of the character's intentions. If you have a character who is unreliable, their use of humour can be a great way to show that.

TURN CONFLICT RESOLUTION UPSIDE DOWN TO INCREASE CONFLICT

In my previous day job, one of my duties was to do presentations on conflict resolution for different organizations. I would travel around and give talks so that adults in the workplace could learn to play well with one another. I can say that regardless of the office environment, one of the most polarizing issues is people who microwave fish in the lunchroom. Just don't. Trust me. Even if your co-workers haven't said anything, they hate you for it. Also, throw away your lunch leftovers—don't put them back in the fridge to become a failed science experiment.

I realized that while identifying ways to reduce conflict is great for the office, it's also great for fiction. Writers could use those same tips, turn them upside down, and increase the conflict on the page. Let's review possible ways to put this in place in your manuscript, by looking at a common conflict resolution "rule" and then turning it upside down.

Choose the right atmosphere / choose the worst place possible

In real life, you want to choose the best environment to have a difficult conversation. You want to choose a place where the individual can focus on what you are saying and not instantly feel defensive, trapped or uncomfortable. If someone is at ease, they are more receptive to what's being said. In fiction, try to set the conflict in the most *uncomfortable* place possible for your characters.

The uncomfortable location will depend in part on your character. For some characters it may be a fancy restaurant; for another, their in-laws' living room. For almost all of us, a conflict that occurs in a public place is automatically worse than one that occurs in private, in part because we run the risk of other people watching the situation go down. Conflict is almost always inherently awkward, and most of us don't want to show our gawky side in public. There's a reason someone who doesn't want a "scene" when they break up with someone will tell them in a public place. (Of course, these days they simply ghost them.)

When thinking of where to place a conflict, consider not only the physical space, but also who else is present. A friend was once getting ready for a family vacation that would require a week of driving cross-country. The kids were in the car, the suitcases filled the trunk, and she was just grabbing the cooler full of road snacks when her husband told her that when they got back from the trip, he wanted to move out and get a divorce. Then he got in the car.

Personally, I'm somewhat shocked she didn't kill him by clubbing him with the cooler and then running him over with the car. The conflict was worse because her kids were in the back seat, so she couldn't have a discussion with him then and there. And in the evenings, they were staying with relatives. She felt compelled to have a happy vacation for her children, all the while knowing when they returned home her carefully plotted life was going to blow up.

The last piece to consider is *when* the conflict occurs. Imagine you have a scene where the main character's best friend admits she kissed or had sex with the main character's partner. When would be the worst time for this revelation to come out? A few months before the wedding? The night before? How about in the back of the church? Or even more horrible—in front of the church with all her family and friends gathered around to hear the news, too!

Your Turn

- Review where your conflict scenes occur. Is there a setting for these that would create more conflict?
- In what places is your character is most uncomfortable?
- Is there anyone around when the conflict occurs? Could you add anyone?
- When does the conflict occur? Would it benefit the conflict to make it happen sooner or later?

Address issues promptly and directly / let situations build

While it is better for your relationships to address problem areas before they build up, in fiction a pressure build-up is preferred. In real life, we encourage people to speak up when things bother them, perhaps not instantly, but certainly if the problem isn't likely to go away on its own. Otherwise, it'll just keep building until you explode.

On the other hand, exploding is exactly what we want to happen in our manuscripts. Let characters stew until they suddenly erupt with emotion.

We encourage people to clearly state the issue that is bothering them, ideally using "I versus You" language: *"When you leave your dishes in the sink instead of putting them away, it makes me feel like you think it is my job to keep up the home. I get angry when we fall into these traditional roles since I also work full time."*

However, people are rarely this clear. They either don't say anything at all, or they dance around the topic. In the example above, they might say, "Ugh, you're such a pig!" They insult or upset the other person when what really upsets them is that they feel they're being taken advantage of. The other person might counter with, "Just because I'm not OCD about every mote of dust doesn't mean I'm messy. And calling me a pig? Was that some kind of comment on my weight?" Commence giant fight about how clean to keep the house. Except that the person wasn't really upset about the dishes at all—they were afraid of what the dirty dishes meant.

In Chapter Eight, I talked about Rational Emotive Therapy. The impact of beliefs often come up in this area and can lead to conflict, because we're not clear what our beliefs are. For example, someone I'm dating can't believe I hijacked the conversation at a dinner with their boss. I'm upset because I thought I was being charming, and I hadn't even wanted to go to the darn event. I may believe that he thinks that I came across badly and embarrassed him. However, my date might really be worried that his boss doesn't see him as assertive enough, and he doesn't want to be overshadowed by someone so clearly delightful and smart. A large fight may ensue, but it doesn't address the real issue because we're not disclosing—perhaps we're not even aware of—what is truly upsetting us.

Your Turn

- Where can your character bring up an issue, but not the *real* issue? What are they fighting about— and what are they *really* fighting about?
- Do both sides of the conflict know that it isn't the real argument?

Maintain emotional control / lose control

Conflict is contagious. It's like a cold in an elementary school; it spreads like wildfire. If someone raises their voice, the other person is much more likely to increase their volume as well. If one person escalates by swearing, the other person will typically match them. The more emotional people become, the more likely they are to lash out or say something they regret. We tend to meet each other where we are, so if one person is becoming more upset, the other person will ramp it up, too.

This is why, in real life, we encourage people to remain calm whenever possible. It makes it easier for you to attend to what is being said and decreases the chance that things will escalate unnecessarily.

In fiction, you can look for opportunities to spin things completely out of control! Instead of listening and reflecting on what's said, allow your characters to lash out as soon as they disagree with a point, even if the point hasn't been fully expressed. Because they are already formulating a response instead of listening, they are more likely to misunderstand what the other person is trying to say. Conflict is raised one step at a time, and the more emotional the characters become, the more quickly they move up these steps.

Your characters may have triggers, issues, phrases or topics that make them go from zero to one hundred. This may be something from their past, or something that makes them feel vulnerable. For example, if I say to one person, "You're acting just like your mother," they may simply shrug. Another person might hear that and come out screaming.

I once was having an argument with my ex. He looked at me as I tried to explain why I was so upset and said, "You're getting really worked up about this." It was at that moment that the top of my head lifted off and I may have said something like, "You haven't seen worked up," before my head spun around completely and I ripped his intestines out with my teeth. If you know your character's backstory, you know what things are particularly upsetting to them. Hitting them where they feel vulnerable will make them lift off.

Also keep in mind that characters may respond differently to the escalation of an argument. While people will typically match the intensity of a conflict, those who are very conflict averse, or who have dealt with abuse, may back down quickly if things heat up. This doesn't mean the conflict is resolved. In fact, the person who capitulated may feel simmering anger and resentment—and that emotion will come out somewhere at some time.

Your Turn

- What does it look like when your character loses control? Do they cry, scream, silently plot revenge, resort to violence? Create a list.
- What things are most upsetting to your character in an argument? Are there any triggers that make them more likely to lose control?
- Does your character know the other person's triggers? Do they push them on purpose?

Avoid accusations / let those accusations fly

We're hard-wired to believe that we're the hero of our own life story. We find ways to justify our own actions. Yes, we might have lied, but we had a *really* good reason. When we're accused of something, we have a knee-jerk reaction to defend ourselves—to explain that, in fact, the other person was so totally wrong we can hardly believe it. This is why when we teach conflict resolution, we encourage people to use "I" statements and to avoid absolutes like "always" and "never." As soon as someone says, "You always interrupt me!" the other person flashes through every interaction in their memory to find a time when they didn't. They won't even hear or acknowledge the rest of what the other person is saying because they are so consumed with the desire to explain that they don't do it *every* time.

Fiction should follow the opposite rules. Characters should use "you" statements, not "I" statements, and they should throw around *always* and *never* like they're going out of style. Doing this will almost instantly get the other character's back up. The reader will also be more engaged, especially if they identify with the character being accused. They will mentally stiffen and think, "Hey now, that's not fair. [Character name] is not like that!"

Your Turn

⊙ What might your character accuse the other person of doing?

- What accusation would be most hurtful to your character?
- Are there opportunities in your manuscript for a character to default to accusations and absolutes?

Don't hit below the belt / hit below the belt

You've likely heard the saying, "We always hurt the ones we love." Why is that? Because we can. The better we know them, the better we know where to stick the sword. We know their hot buttons. We know what will rile that person up. We may say things that are deliberately hurtful because we feel safe enough to push them, or perhaps we want to test how much they really love us.

However, there are some things that cannot be unsaid. Once those words are out, they're like a steaming pile in the middle of your living room. You can clean it up and spray some air freshener around, but everyone still knows the stink is there.

If one character tells another, "Yes, the person I had an affair with is better than you in bed," they can apologize over and over, but I'm willing to bet the other character will never forget it. If a character says, "If your mom knew what you'd done, she would be so ashamed of you," the other character is going to carry that around as a tiny nugget of pain and resentment.

Hitting below the belt means hitting where someone is most vulnerable. It's an area where it is hard to protect ourselves, and where even a glancing blow feels much worse. Most often, if you're hitting someone below the belt, you're doing it because you want to cause some damage.

In fiction, this allows you not only to increase the conflict, but also to show where your character is most vulnerable. And if your character is the one hitting below the belt, it will also demonstrate their personality. The reader typically won't like a character who does this, or at the very least they will want the character to feel bad for having inflicted that kind of damage. (Although they may, on the other hand, be impressed with that character's ability to be truly nasty.)

Your Turn

- What could someone say about your character that would be deeply painful for them?
- What could your character say about someone else that would be deeply painful?
- If your character does hit below the belt, how do they feel about it? Proud of themselves? Guilty?
- Look at your manuscript and make notes where the characters could have an "oh no, you didn't" moment.

Don't focus on the past / drag the past back into the present

If a situation has been resolved, you shouldn't keep bringing it up into the present. Unless it's fiction, of course, in which case this can be a great place to bring in interesting backstory! Drag that carcass of past arguments and personal information right back onto the page for us all to get a good look at.

In real life, when you constantly bring up things from the past, you're not allowing someone to move forward. In fiction, however, bringing up the past can heighten the present situation and provide context. It can allow us to see if characters have patterns of behaviour or what may have transpired between them in the past. It also shows the reader aspects of the character's past that may be relevant to their current motivations or the current plot.

For example, you may have a scene where one teen is angry at their parent. They state that the parent never cared about them. (This is best said really dramatically, with an emphasis on *never*.) The child brings up the time when the parent was several hours late to pick them up from school. This may be relevant because:

- the teen has issues around feeling abandoned;
- there's a history of neglect;
- the parent is ashamed because as a single parent, they are often barely holding it together; or
- they didn't show up because they are actually in the witness protection agency and a former spy,

and once again they fear their cover has been blown. Commence chase scenes and drama.

Your Turn

- Bringing up the past in an argument provides a great place to insert backstory in an interesting way. If your manuscript contains an info dump, but you want to keep in that information, is it possible to add the revelation to a conflict scene?
- What would your character least like to have brought up in an argument? Is there a way to do that?

Allies, enemies, and the art of bringing others into the fight

When I used to teach conflict resolution, I would talk about the importance of not enlisting an army to make your case. It can feel good to show that others support what you're saying or doing. It's nice to have people on your side. However, if you're on the other side, it feels an awful lot like people ganging up on you. And it can be really hurtful if there are people you never expected to see on the other side.

In fiction, however, pulling in other characters allows you accomplish several things:

- It allows you to up the emotional stakes by showing the seeming betrayal of people the character trusts.
- It shows the larger challenge the character faces— it's not just one person who opposes them, but a team.
- It illustrates the different sides or teams involved in a particular conflict.

Your Turn

- Who would your character want on their side in an argument?
- Who would your character dread to see on the opposite side?

Creating win-win situations / creating a loser in the situation

In real-life conflict resolution situations, we encourage people to search out areas of common ground. This allows each party to gain something from the solution. In fiction, we want to keep our character's focus not on what they have in common with each other, but what sets them apart. If your character equates giving ground with losing something, they will fight to win rather than compromise.

This is huge. The more a character stands to lose or win— the more it counts—the further they will go to the mat to get it. It means the character will push forward no matter what you throw at them, and let's be honest—you're going to throw a lot at them. It's so important, that in the next chapter, I discuss *stakes*.

Your Turn

⊙ What does your character stand to lose if they lose this conflict? What is at risk?

WHAT'S AT STAKE?

If we see conflict as win-lose versus win-win, then there will be a character that comes out on top and one that doesn't. One will have the outcome they were pursuing, and the other won't. The conflict is all about who will emerge the victor, which means something is at stake for *each* of the characters.

What happens if your character *doesn't* get what they want, if the conflict bests them? These are the stakes. This is what is being risked.

Life-or-death

Life-or-death stakes are the easiest to imagine. If you don't figure out how to defuse the bomb in x number of seconds (and counting down with every single breath), then it will go off. You'll die. Likely other people in the scene will die, maybe even someone you love or, god forbid, the dog. Or perhaps in this story you are going for broke—the bomb will destroy the *entire planet*. Heck, why not take out the known universe while you're at it? All the writer has to do is build a bigger bomb.

With life-or-death stakes, the character must win the conflict or risk being hacked in half by a lightsaber, eaten by a dragon, consumed by fire or zombies, frozen to death, sucked into space or any other scenario that concludes in a big *game over*.

These are stakes a reader can easily understand. They will feel tension, their heartbeat may accelerate, their muscles could clench, a thick sense of dread may grow in their stomach and, most importantly, they will be turning those pages like crazy to find out what happens so they can alleviate that tension. After all, someone's *life* is on the line.

Life-or-death also means that the character is willing to do most anything to get through the situation. The desire to survive is a strong one. I hate bugs and spiders. This is a massive understatement. I once stayed in my car for several hours until someone else could come to my house and get rid of a large (freakishly large if you ask me, like, doused-in-radiation large) spider that I had trapped under a glass. I didn't want to be in the house with the trapped spider because if it tipped over the glass in a bid to escape, I didn't want to be nearby when it sought revenge. However, despite this very rational phobia, if you said that I would be shot if I did not lie down and let spiders crawl on me, I'd assume the corpse pose. Because I want to keep living.

To be clear, I really, really, *really* wouldn't want to do it. I would attempt to come up with any other possible solution. But if the choice was to be shot or to face down those eight-legged hell creatures, I'd take the spiders— even if I ended up with serious PTSD and a tendency to have nightmares for the rest of my life.

If you push your character up to this wall, it becomes very interesting to see how far they would go. Face down spiders? Yes. Kill someone else? I don't know. I'd like to think I wouldn't take someone else's life just to save my own, and I hope never to be in a situation where I have to find out. In my own fiction, one of the things I've explored is if someone would carry out a murder plot if the stakes were high enough.

In the *Hunger Games*, Katniss is in a life-or-death situation. She must survive in the arena or die—and to survive, she must kill those she is competing against. However, over the course of the book (and movie), her experiences change her. While initially her goal is simply survival, by the climax of the book, she is more interested in a fundamental "right." When the government tells her in the final twist that she must kill Peeta or be killed, she puts her foot down. She and Peeta agree that they'd rather enter a suicide pact than hurt each other, if that's what it takes. They become, at that moment, revolutionaries, willing to lay down their lives for an issue they feel is important.

Many war stories contain an element of self-sacrifice. Soldiers head into battle, a life-or-death conflict. They want to win. However, they will put their own lives at risk (running directly at a machine gun turret, for example) if it means their side's overall objective is met. Space pilots aim their ship into another to save their friends. Police, firefighters and military personnel often risk their own lives for a greater good.

Non-life-or-death stakes

Before you throw your keyboard up in despair because your story doesn't have life-or-death stakes, hang on. You don't need to add zombies, Darth Vader or a rogue sociopath to have good conflict. Many novels have conflict that isn't about survival.

However, while you do not need to include life-or-death stakes, it must *feel* like life-or-death to the character.

There are a lot of things in life that I want. For example, I love a good pair of shoes. (This is another understatement.) However, rarely do I feel that getting a particular pair is a life-or-death event. If I see a pair I love and discover they cost $5,000, I put them (carefully) back down on the display, perhaps kissing them softly first, and then walk away. I don't take a second job, miss a house payment, or risk possible jail time by shoving them in my bag and running full speed toward the door, screaming, "You'll never catch me, coppers!"

I *want* the shoes. I don't *need* the shoes.

However, I could create a plot where owning those shoes feels vital. Perhaps I've convinced myself that those shoes will bring me infinite confidence. If I had those shoes, I could rock an upcoming presentation. And that presentation is the key to getting that big promotion. If I

Want vs. need

got the promotion, I could pay off the debt hanging over my head. And if I were free of that debt, I could finally turn my attention to having a family. All of a sudden, getting those shoes is about a lot more than how beautiful they are. They matter. Those shoes are what stand between a life of loneliness and regret and a happy family life.

This larger-than-life thinking also works in the reverse. I was a high-strung kid. Anxiety and I were in a close relationship. I was a good student, but despite the fact I did well in school it was still a huge source of stress for me. Once my mother caught me crying in my bedroom and tried to determine what had me so upset. I admitted that I had a test coming up. I was afraid I wouldn't do well. And if I didn't do well on the test, I wouldn't do well in the class. And if I didn't do well in the class, I wouldn't get into a good university. And if I didn't get into university, I wouldn't get a good job. And if I didn't get a good job, then I'd likely end up homeless, wearing men's shoes and a worn sweater that smelled like cat pee.

This made *total* sense to me. I'm pretty sure my mom was less clear on the connection between a test in the morning and a life of dumpster diving. To me, the stakes of doing well on that test mattered deeply.

What is at stake for your character is less important than making sure the reader understands the connection between what's at stake and why it matters to that particular character. The character places meaning on those non-life-threatening stakes. They will perceive a consequence which may, or may not, be easy to follow. For one character, losing the school bake-off may mean that she's not a good mom. For another, not figuring out how to negotiate with a reptilian alien race may prove their dad was right and they'll never amount to anything.

Downsides to raising the stakes

Hopefully I've convinced you to create stakes that matter for your conflict and characters. But is there such thing as too much?

With life-or-death stakes, there's a risk that if the reader cannot follow or feel the impact of the danger the character faces, they will stop caring. The reader may feel like it was a fun ride, but a novel isn't a Disney ride.

Let's consider a Disney ride for a moment.

As a rite of passage, my amusement park–hating parents took to me to Disney World as a kid. Looking back, I can only imagine the horror of entering a giant theme park complete with giant dancing characters for my quiet, bookish parents. They clearly loved me.

One of the rides I forced them to go on multiple times was the Pirates of the Caribbean. For me, it was the happy medium—it featured a few scary moments, but I never felt like I wanted to throw up like I did on Space Mountain. (If, in the late 70s, someone puked on you during that ride, my apologies. It might have been me.)

On the Pirates ride, you bumped and meandered through the various rooms in a small boat, gawking at pirates playing, battling, and yo-ho-hoing here and there. But when they decided to make *Pirates of the Caribbean* into a movie, they had to create *characters*. Enter the divine performances of Johnny Depp as Jack Sparrow, Keira Knightley as Elizabeth Swann and Orlando Bloom as Will Turner. They created backstories and motivations for each of the characters that carry them through the battles, play, and yo-ho-hoing. It was a fun visual spectacle, and while I'm not going to argue that it was an Oscar-worthy screenplay, the movie works because we care about the people in the story. If the movie were nothing more than a stationary "ride" through sets and scenes—things blowing up, ships sinking, some great swordplay—it wouldn't have worked. A ride works for a few minutes. You won't get bored. However, a ride will become dull if it lasts as long it takes to read a complete novel.

If you don't have an emotional connection to the people in the story, then the characters are nothing more than plot devices. The reader may not use that term to define them, but worse than that, they simply won't care.

Your Turn

- What is at stake for your character if they do not win their conflict?
- Is there anything or anyone for which they would lay down their life? Is there a greater good?
- If the stakes *are* life-or-death, what is the emotional impact? That is, why does this conflict matter to them beyond simply the need to survive?
- If the stakes are not life-or-death, what meaning do

they put on the stakes to make it feel like life-or-death to them?

- Write a journal entry from the POV of your main character that addresses what it would be like if they don't win.
- Take time to understand the stakes from all your characters' points of view. Consider not only what your main character has at risk, but also your antagonist. If they're also well motivated, it will drive the story forward.

12

MOTIVATION

The concept of motivation has come up a few times in this book and is essential to understanding conflict. Without motivation, people will give up when faced with conflict. That's just smart. For example, I'm walking down the street and there's a huge puddle. *Huge.* Likely with worms in it. And mud that will get on my shoes. (And I have good shoes.)

Confronted with this vast, worm-filled puddle, I'll walk around it. If it's so big that I can't get around it, I might decide to turn around and go home. I can go out for a walk some other time when I'm not going to end up with muddy, worm-filled shoes and wet feet. If you want me to stomp through a puddle, then you'd better give me a good reason. Perhaps the bus I need to catch is just about to leave. Or my dog has gotten off of his leash and is running toward a busy road. Or Ryan Reynolds is up ahead, handing out fresh-baked snickerdoodle cookies.

And this is just a puddle. Imagine how much larger a character's motivation would have to be for them to face the conflict in your book. Puddles and worms are one thing. Zombies are a whole other level of fear. And falling in love after a heartbreak? I think I might prefer the zombies or worms, or zombies *with* worms.

If you want a character to venture outside their comfort zone, you need to give them a really good reason to step out there—and an even better reason to continue when they get knocked down in their pursuit.

As a counsellor, I know that motivation can take the form of a push or a pull. To explain this concept, my book *Build Better Characters* used the example of an individual standing on top of a skyscraper. Would they jump from the roof, one hundred stories up, to the building next door?

Generally, the answer is no unless they have dreams of extreme parkour. However, a push motivation would be to tell the individual that the building they're standing on is on fire and the only way to survive is to make the jump. A pull motivation would be to point at something amazing on the roof of the other building, like a pile of money that is free for the taking. In the puddle example above, the prospect of missing my bus is a push. Dreamy Ryan Reynolds passing out cookies is an example of a pull (and my overactive imagination).

You need to know why your character wants to achieve their goal so that when things pile up against them, they will continue. That's their motivation.

What motivates your character may evolve and change over the course of the story. For example, they may start with a motivation that is self-directed but over the course of the story start to believe in a higher cause. In the first *Star Wars* movie (Episode IV), Han Solo initially agrees to assist in the rescue of Princess Leia because he's being paid well to do it. By the end of the movie, he joins the effort to destroy the Death Star not for the money but because he's come to care about the other characters. He's invested in their cause and now is a part of the rebellion, even though it means risking his life and ship. This represents a huge character shift for him, and this change continues in *The Empire Strikes Back*.

Your Turn

- What is your character's motivation in the book?
- Does this motivation change?
- How can you make this motivation even more important to them? Are they pushed or pulled or both?

HOW TO MEASURE CONFLICT IN YOUR MANUSCRIPT

I'm often asked, "How do you know if you have enough conflict in your book?" This is one of those questions that is darn hard to answer for someone else. You need to have enough to keep your readers engaged. However, that will vary depending on the type of story you're working on. The amount of conflict needed for an international story of espionage is different than that for a story of a mother learning to let her disabled child have their independence. The types of conflict will vary. Hopefully this book has given you a lot of ways to explore conflict in *your* story. If one conflict strategy doesn't work for your book, hopefully another will.

It is important to understand where conflict exists in your story. There are those who argue that every scene must contain some sort of conflict. I tend to agree. However, it seems as soon as I make this argument, some student is able to think of a scene in a vastly successful novel that doesn't have any conflict. As a result, while I won't insist that it needs to be in every scene—although it's a good challenge to see if you can get it in there—you're better off to have it more often than not.

One way to determine this is to break down the goal, motivation and conflict in each scene. For a more in-depth understanding of these concepts, consider Debra Dixon's *Goal, Motivation, Conflict*. For each scene in your novel, look at each character and ask yourself, "What do they want? Why do they want it? What keeps them from getting it?"

I like to go old-school with my manuscripts and bust out some index cards. (Be still, my heart. How I love thee, office supplies.) For each scene, I use an index card to list:

- chapter number,
- characters who appear in the scene,
- scene location and time (if relevant), and
- a bulleted list of scene events.

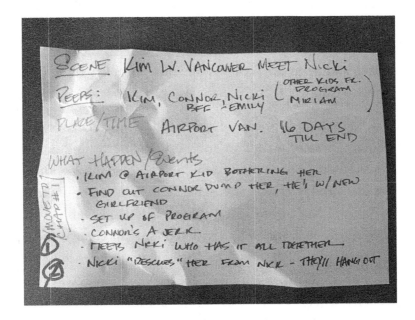

At the top of the card, I place a plus or minus to indicate if the scene opens on a positive or negative note, and I do the same at the bottom of the card to show how it ends. Then I place a number from one to ten in a small circle to indicate the level of conflict in that scene, with one denoting a minor conflict or annoyance and ten denoting a full-on war.

I then lay out all the cards on a table or corkboard. This allows me to see my story in a linear, visual format. (Be aware that while I like this old-school way, software programs like Scrivener offer fancy, high-tech ways to do this. *Strategic Series Author* by Crystal Hunt describes several programs that help outline and track information both for series and stand-alone novels.)

What I am looking for with the big picture is a "heartbeat" running through the story, a rise and fall, like an EKG rhythm of tension and conflict in the story. Am I giving the character—and the reader—a chance to catch their breath, reflect and regroup so they can face the next thing I'm going to throw at them?

It's the back and forth, rise and fall that helps engage the reader. It creates a rhythm and keeps them turning pages to see what happens. For example, if you have a favourite perfume and you wear it daily, there will come a time when you don't even smell it anymore. However, if you have a couple scents that you like, and you change them up every so often, you don't have an opportunity to become "nose blind" to them. Conflict is that way for readers. If you keep it always the same, they become immune to it, even if you're blowing things up on every page. After a while, they won't even flinch.

But if you change it up, you'll keep readers on their toes.

How can you change it up?

- After periods of high conflict, provide an opportunity for characters to reflect and catch their breath.
- Switch between internal and external conflict in scenes.
- Change the source of the conflict. Perhaps in one scene it's nature, and in another it's a bad guy.
- Vary the intensity of the conflict from one to ten.
- Switch up how well your character responds to conflict, from coping well to falling apart.
- At times, have your character succeed when faced with conflict. At other times, have them fail.

Your Turn

- Consider using the notecard exercise to track conflict levels in your own manuscript.
- Are there ways you can vary the type and intensity of your conflict?

CONCLUSION

Hopefully I've convinced you that conflict is essential to making your manuscript work and provided you with some options on how to rile up your characters and create some conflict. Maybe you've thrown in a bear attack, or some nagging self-doubt (both can be crippling.) Conflict is something that you can return to again and again as you work on your manuscript. If you're a member of The Creative Academy we talk about it frequently in my office hours. (Not a member? Why the heck not? Joining is free! Find us here: https://creativeacademyforwriters.com/

For a specific list of office hours and masterclasses on conflict, visit the resources page for this book at:

http://creativeacademyforwriters.com/ resources/createstoryconflict/

Be brave enough to challenge your character and you'll have readers madly flipping pages until the very end so they can share in that celebration of victory.

MORE CREATIVE ACADEMY GUIDES FOR WRITERS

More Creative Academy Guides for Writers

We've got a whole series of books to help you along your writing and publishing journey.

Available in eBook & print!

Scrappy Rough Draft by Donna Barker
Build Better Characters by Eileen Cook

Strategic Series Author by Crystal Hunt
Create Story Conflict by Eileen Cook
Strategic AuthorPreneur by Crystal Hunt
Full Time Author by Eileen Cook + Crystal Hunt
Connect With Readers by Crystal Hunt

If you'd like an email notification each time we release a new title in this series, click here and get thee on our mailing list.

ACKNOWLEDGMENTS

As anyone who has ever attempted to write a book knows, it ain't easy. Real life has a tendency to get in the way—and that's not even counting things like Netflix or staring vacantly into space, which often seem like a better use of time. I'm well aware that the reason you're holding this book at all is because I'm smart enough to surround myself with the right people, who offer both encouragement and butt kicking in necessary amounts.

First off, I have to thank the team at The Creative Academy. These amazing writers are all pushing forward on their own journey, but they still find time to help each other. They inspire me every day. They ask me challenging questions during office hours, which leads to things like this book. Plus, they can be counted on to ask the annoying question, "So when is that book going to be done?" which makes me keen to meet the deadline and give them an answer.

My partners in crime, Donna Barker and Crystal Hunt, are the kind of women I always dreamed of working with. They're funny, kind, brilliant, strategic, and unlikely to put up with any bullshit. There's no doubt that this book is better because of them. Oh, who am I kidding? Without them, I'd still be sitting on the sofa, watching Netflix and talking about how I should write a craft book on conflict one of these days.

Elissa McColl, Jenny Graham-Lang, and Brenda Murphy were beta readers who offered their time and energy to make this better. Big thanks.

Thank you to the readers of my previous book, *Build Better Characters*. They suggested subjects they wanted to learn more about and indicated that conflict was a topic they wanted to explore in more detail. I appreciate their input and support. If you have ideas that you'd like a future book to address, please feel free to reach out to me— eileen@creativeacademyforwriters.com.

My dogs, by their mere existence, mean that I'm not wandering around talking to myself. They willingly listen as I grapple with things out loud, especially if I provide treats. Plus, because they need a walk, I'm occasionally required to put on grown-up clothing and go outside, which is likely good for me.

Lastly, I want to acknowledge and thank *you*. Writing is a lonely task. Knowing that someone will be reading these words provides that important connection. I know how many great writing craft books are out there—I own most of them—so I appreciate you giving this book your time and energy. I truly hope it helps move your writing to the next level.

LIST OF RESOURCES

Build Better Characters: The psychology of backstory & how to use it in your writing to hook readers by Eileen Cook, Creative Academy for Writers, 2019

Characters, Emotion & Viewpoint by Nancy Kress, Writer's Digest Books, 2005

Goal, Motivation, and Conflict by Debra Dixon, Gryphon Books for Writers, 2013

Scrappy Rough Draft: Use science to strategically motivate yourself & finish writing your book by Donna Barker, Creative Academy for Writers, 2019

Strategic Series Author: Plan, write and publish a series to maximize readership & income by Crystal Hunt, Creative Academy for Writers, 2019

The Emotion Thesaurus: A Writer's Guide to Character Expression, 2nd edition by Angela Ackerman and Becca Puglisi, JADD Publishing, 2019

The Science of Positivity: Stop Negative Thought Patterns by Changing Your Brain Chemistry by Loretta Graziano Breuning, Adams Media, 2016

Writing Screenplays that Sell, 20th edition, by Michael Hauge, Collins Reference, 2011

Writing the Breakout Novel: Winning Advice from a Top Agent and His Best-selling Client by Donald Maass, Writer's Digest Books, 2002

YOUR TURNS ALL IN ONE PLACE

You can download a PDF of all the Your Turn exercises from the resources page for this book at http://creativeacademyforwriters.com/resources/createstoryconflict/

Chapter One

When we talk about conflict, we might not mean the same thing

- I firmly believe that one of the best ways for writers to improve their craft is to be careful readers. Take the time to reread one of your favourite books. In every chapter, attempt to identify the conflict and use sticky notes or a highlighter to mark those conflicts. (I know some people believe marking up books is a great sin. What can I say? I'm a rebel.) When you've finished reading, go back through the conflicts again. Put a check mark if they are external conflicts and a star if they are internal. Lastly, look at how the conflict builds in the story, and how it impacts the character and the plot.

- You can also do this exercise with movies, TV dramas, half-hour sitcoms and, in some cases, commercials. Stories come in all shapes and sizes, so be open to exploring conflict in all forms.
- Listen when people tell stories about what happened to them. These may be work issues, a car breakdown, an interaction with a spouse or what happened on their vacation. How many of these stories include some kind of conflict? How does that impact your interest in hearing what happened?

Why is conflict so important in fiction?

- Journal about a time you were under a lot of pressure or facing a lot of conflict. How did you behave or respond? What did your response show about your character?
- Journal about a time someone you knew was in a difficult situation. Did they respond well or poorly? Were you ever shocked by what you learned about that individual?
- Is there a struggle that your character looks back on fondly, impressed with what they got through? Conversely, is there something in their past they aren't proud of?

Chapter Two

Types of conflict

- Does your manuscript have external conflict? What kind?
- Does your manuscript have internal conflict? What are the things at war within the character?
- Perhaps your book has a bit of both types of conflict. If there is only one, is there an opportunity to add some more? (Never fear—I'm going to give you some ideas below.)

Sources of external conflict

Weather and nature

- Do you have any nature conflicts in your story? If not, is there room to add to conflict by making the world around your character turn against them?
- If you're writing a historical novel, have you researched to see if any major weather events occurred during the time your story covers?
- If you're writing a fantasy or science-fiction novel, have you determined how nature functions in this new world? Are there rules?
- How does the weather support your story or theme?

Social and systemic conflict

- What is the society within which your character

functions? (Consider the overarching one, but also the smaller "sub-societies" they are a part of.)

- List the rules of the society in your manuscript. Next to each rule (which may be unspoken), indicate if your main character agrees with it or not.
- What beliefs and values does the society hold? What do they see as important? Later in this book, we'll be discussing character values, so there may be an opportunity to put character and society values in conflict.

Setting

- What is the first thing that comes to your mind when you think of a place where your character would feel most comfortable? Least comfortable?
- Look at the scene settings in your novel. Are there any you could change to maximize the conflict?
- Consider how descriptions of a setting change the feel. Take five to ten minutes to describe the space you are in at the moment. Then take another five to ten minutes to describe the same space, but imagine you're writing a horror novel. Then take yet another five or ten minutes and describe the setting through the eyes of someone who has time-travelled to that space from the 1700s. What things would someone in a horror novel notice—the looming bookcase, threatening to bury them alive? What would the time traveller notice—the odd flame-free device that gives off no heat but is still so bright?

- How could changing the setting in your novel make things worse for your character or increase the opportunity for conflict?
- Look at the sensory details in a place that makes them uncomfortable. How can you highlight these? What are the smells and textures?
- Is your character in a relationship with someone who feels exactly the opposite in that setting?

A bad guy (or creature)

- Why does your bad guy want to stop your main character? What is it that they want in the book and why do they want it? Are there people who would agree with them?
- Write a journal entry from your villain's point of view that explains what they find annoying, challenging, or rage-inducing about your character.
- Pull out some of your favourite books and look at the bad guy (or girl). What makes them interesting?
- If you were to turn your story upside down—the way *Wicked* tells the *Wizard of Oz* from the Wicked Witch's perspective—how would your bad guy tell the story?

A good guy (or creature) who wants the same as your character

- Consider a time in your life when a friend or

family member was in the pursuit of the same thing you were. How did you feel?

- Would it be worse for your character to be opposed by someone they normally go to for support?
- Is there a character in your book who would normally be on their side, but in this instance—this very, very, very important instance—is on the opposite side?

Make them worthy of your protagonist

- On a scale of one to ten, where one is weak and ten is Darth Vader–level badassery, where does your antagonist fall? Are they bad enough to make your protagonist really have to stretch in order to be successful?
- Create a list of your protagonist's strengths and weaknesses. Then list your antagonist's strengths and weaknesses. How well-matched are they? In what situations is one stronger than the other? Is there a way that your antagonist can be extra strong in a way your protagonist is extra weak?

Chapter Three

Internal Conflict

Competing wants

- Consider a past goal that was difficult to reach or that you abandoned. What stopped you from reaching that goal? Were any of these obstacles internal? Did you use an external obstacle as an excuse? What competing wants did you face? For example, if you goal was to complete university and you dropped out, was it because your parents refused to pay for school if you pursued something "silly" like creative writing? That's an external reason. But if you dig deep, there were ways around this barrier. You could have changed majors. You could have taken out loans. You could have worked part time and gone to school part time. What was happening internally that kept you from trying one of these alternatives? The goal of this exercise isn't to beat yourself up or make yourself feel bad. (Or to drive you into therapy, for that matter). The goal is to recognize that what often prevents us from reaching our goals is what we tell ourselves.

- What is the primary goal that drives your character? What competing wants might they have? How can you show these in your manuscript?
- Does your character acknowledge these competing wants, or are they in denial?
- Is your character able to identify both external and internal impacts on their goal?
- What does your character's inner voice tell them about what they want? Does it whisper "you've got this" or "you'll never amount to anything"?

Values and beliefs

- Make a list of your character's values. If you need some suggestions, consider this list:

Authenticity

Adventure

Authority

Autonomy

Balance

Beauty

Boldness

Bravery

Calm

Compassion

Community

Common Sense

Creativity

Curiosity

Dignity

Equality

Fairness

Faith

Fame

Family

Friendships

Freedom

Fun

Growth

Happiness

Honesty

Honour

Independence

Justice

Kindness

Knowledge

Leadership

Learning

Logic

Love

Loyalty

Openness

Optimism

Peace

Pleasure

Popularity

Recognition

Religion

Reputation

Respect

Responsibility

Security

Self-Respect

Service

Spirituality

Stability

Success

Status

Timeliness

Trustworthiness

Wealth

Wisdom

- Choose five of these for your character. Select three as the most important to your character. Consider where each of those values came from, and what happened to your character to make them embrace those values as central to their lives.

The impact of character arc

- What might need to happen for your character to act against their values?
- If you character is experiencing a change in their values, what is causing that change? How can you show it by going back and forth between the two values?
- Have you ever been in a situation or relationship that created a clash in your values? When did you become aware of the conflict? How did you resolve it? Dig deep, and journal on how you felt about this clash.

Chapter Four

How to build tension

Create an emotional connection

- Pull two or three of your favourite books off the shelf (or pick a favourite TV show or movie). Write the name of the main character at the top of the page and then a journal entry about why you care about that person.
- Imagine that you are a TV producer and you want to foster interest in a story about what happens to your main character. What would you want the audience to know in order to get them emotionally involved in the story?

Give your reader more information than you give the protagonist

- Draw a line down the centre of a sheet of paper. On one side, write down what the main character knows in a particular scene. On the other side, show what the reader (or you, the author) knows. Is there a way to build tension by hiding something from your character?
- Fix Ellen up with a sexy science guy to see what happens. (Okay, that's not really a writing exercise, but I'm interested to hear how it turns out. Then you can write about it. It's a win-win thing. English accent not required—I'll also accept Irish, Scottish, Italian... heck, pretty much anything.)

Up the stakes

- What is at risk for your character in the scene?
- What will happen if your character doesn't take the action they do?

Create a background for tension

- Look at a scene that appears just *before* a high-conflict moment in your manuscript. Does it give the reader any clues that something may be about to happen?
- Review your sensory description in tense or conflicted scenes. Are you getting the biggest bang out of them? Instead of something smelling sour, perhaps there is a scent of decay. Is there a noise

just barely audible, almost like someone is whispering a warning?

Chapter 5

Why do writers sometimes have weak conflict?

- Be honest. Have you gone too easy on your characters with conflict in your manuscript?
- What is the reason you've backed down on pushing the conflict? What is it about conflict that scares you or makes you uncomfortable?
- Create a list of every possible thing that could go wrong for your characters, and don't hold back. Keep thinking of options until you're down to ideas that seem absurd—and then make yourself list at least two more. Sit on those ideas for a couple of days, and then revisit the list. Are there things you can add to your manuscript?
- Reach out to another writer and offer to provide them with conflict ideas for their manuscript if they'll provide ideas for your story. Having someone to chat with about book ideas can be a great support when you need to get outside your head to discover what's working and what isn't.

Chapter Six

Understanding conflict response

Fight

- Does your story include circumstances in which your character has to fight for survival?
- Is their decision to fight a good one? Or do they not understand they're likely to lose?
- What would push your character to finally take a swing at someone?

Flee

- If your character runs from a conflict, how do they feel about that decision? Are they disappointed in themselves?
- How do the people around them view that decision?
- What "injury" (physical, but more likely emotional) do they risk if they fight? What do they risk if they don't take a stand at this point?
- Is your character the lion or the bunny in this fight?

Freeze

- What or who is the T-Rex in your character's life—the one they freeze to avoid?
- How do they feel when they freeze?
- Would your character speak up or stay frozen if they saw someone else attacked?

Fawn

- Does your character ever use fawning as a response to conflict?

- How do they feel about themselves if they do this?
- Does anyone fawn over them? How do they respond?

Chapter Seven

Conflict and characters

- How does your character's family deal with conflict? Are they comfortable with that response?
- If you have two characters in a relationship, consider having them come from families with very different responses to conflict. How will they negotiate what conflict looks like in their relationship?
- What is your character's past experience with conflict? Did it go well?
- Does your character feel their perspective is being heard? Are they hearing others?
- How would your protagonist hurt another character they care about by raising conflict?
- On a scale from one to ten, where one means they have very clear personal boundaries and ten means they are a doormat, how much of a people pleaser is your character?
- How clearly does your character know where they stand on an issue? Are there things they still need to figure out?
- What conflict might your character put off because of a fear of loss? What would they potentially lose if a fight were to happen?
- What does your character already have on their

plate? Are they too exhausted for another argument? Is there something they would normally care a lot about that they currently don't have the energy to cope with?

When conflict avoidance blows up

- Does your character avoid problems but still hang on to their annoyance?
- What past experiences are already in their bag? How large is their bag?
- What will be the issue that makes this finally blow?

The opposite of conflict avoidance

- Does your character believe they are right in almost all situations? How do they cope with people who disagree?
- Are there specific issues that trigger your character? Issues over which they believe anyone who opposes them doesn't simply have another opinion, but is actively wrong?

Overgeneralization

- Have you ever been in an argument about one issue, and the other individual overgeneralized it to include several things that you didn't agree with? How did you respond?
- How can you expand one of your character's conflicts to include more than the issue at hand?

Defence can be the best offence

- Does your character take responsibility for the things they've done, or do they always deny wrongdoing?
- Is there an argument in your manuscript where another character can avoid taking responsibility, leaving your protagonist holding the bag?

Desire for drama

- Does your character have a flair for the dramatic? Do they enjoy conflict because it makes them feel alive?
- Is there someone in your character's life who thrives on drama? How do they react to conflict?
- If your character has a relationship that thrives on conflict, what do they enjoy about it?

Other unhealthy ways to respond to conflict

- Does your character have empathy burnout? What led to this? Write a journal entry about a time in the past when they faced a similar situation but had *all the feels*.
- Does your character ever withhold emotion? What do they tell themselves about why they are doing this?
- If your character is in conflict with someone who withdraws emotion, how does this make them feel? Do they then give in?
- Would you describe any of your characters as

passive aggressive? If your character is passive aggressive, do they know it, or do they think they're behaving innocently? How does this passive aggression show up in their interactions?

- If you character interacts with someone who is passive aggressive, how do they respond?

Healthy ways to manage conflict

- Review the fifteen different aspects of emotional intelligence and identify if your character has specific strengths in any of these areas. How does this help them in conflict situations?
- Does your character have any specific weaknesses in emotional intelligence? How does that impact their ability to cope with conflict?

Chapter Eight

What causes conflict?

Differing needs or wants

- What does your character want in the book? Is it possible for them to also want the opposite?
- Consider characters in your manuscript. Can you put their wants and needs in opposition?

Different ideas or perspectives

- Review the issues in your book. What is your

character's perspective or opinion on these issues? Can you set up another character to oppose this?

Perception of threat

- Identify an activating event in your story. What is your character's belief about that event?
- Is that belief accurate? How does that belief change the consequence?
- Brainstorm a list of possible beliefs your character could have about an activating event. Would any of these lead to a more interesting outcome than the one you currently have?

Stress

- How does your character deal with stress? Do they:
- become agitated or restless?
- lash out at others?
- withdraw?
- become very analytical?
- become very emotional?
- How does that stress show up in their body? Do they:
- pick their nails?
- chew the ends of their hair?
- bite the inside their cheek?
- bounce in place?
- feel nauseated?
- get headaches?

- experience tension across the shoulders (or in other area)?
- If you were to rank your character's stress tolerance on a scale of one to ten—with one meaning they fall apart at the smallest pressure and ten meaning they are calm and collected even during an apocalypse—where does your character fall?
- Prior to the beginning of the book, what was the most stressful event your character ever had to deal with?
- Does your character's stress tolerance change during the book?
- How do the people around them deal with stress?

Chapter Nine

Non-verbal communication and conflict

- Look at a conflict scene in your manuscript. What non-verbal communication is shown on the page? Do the characters recognize what *isn't* being said?
- Challenge yourself to write a conflict scene in which the characters cannot say what they are really angry about. How much can you communicate without any dialogue?

Chapter Ten

Turn conflict resolution upside down to increase conflict

Choose the right atmosphere / choose the worst place possible

- Review where your conflict scenes occur. Is there a setting for these that would create more conflict?
- In what places is your character is most uncomfortable?
- Is there anyone around when the conflict occurs? Could you add anyone?
- When does the conflict occur? Would it benefit the conflict to make it happen sooner or later?

Address issues promptly and directly / let situations build

- Where can your character bring up an issue, but not the *real* issue? What are they fighting about— and what are they *really* fighting about?
- Do both sides of the conflict know that it isn't the real argument?

Maintain emotional control / lose control

- What does it look like when your character loses control? Do they cry, scream, silently plot revenge, resort to violence? Create a list.
- What things are most upsetting to your character in an argument? Are there any triggers that make them more likely to lose control?
- Does your character know the other person's triggers? Do they push them on purpose?

Avoid accusations / let those accusations fly

- What might your character accuse the other person of doing?
- What accusation would be most hurtful to your character?
- Are there opportunities in your manuscript for a character to default to accusations and absolutes?

Don't hit below the belt / hit below the belt

- What could someone say about your character that would be deeply painful for them?
- What could your character say about someone else that would be deeply painful?
- If your character does hit below the belt, how do they feel about it? Proud of themselves? Guilty?
- Look at your manuscript and make notes where the characters could have an "oh no, you didn't" moment.

Don't focus on the past / drag the past back into the present

- Bringing up the past in an argument provides a great place to insert backstory in an interesting way. If your manuscript contains an info dump, but you want to keep in that information, is it possible to add the revelation to a conflict scene?
- What would your character least like to have brought up in an argument? Is there a way to do that?

Allies, enemies, and the art of bringing others into the fight

- Who would your character want on their side in an argument?
- Who would your character dread to see on the opposite side?

Creating win-win situations / creating a loser in the situation

- What does your character stand to lose if they lose this conflict? What is at risk?

Chapter Eleven

What's at stake?

- What is at stake for your character if they do not win their conflict?
- Is there anything or anyone for which they would lay their life? Is there a greater good?
- If the stakes are life-or-death, what is the emotional impact as well? That is, why does this conflict matter to them beyond simply the need to survive?
- If the stakes are not life-or-death, what meaning do they put on the stakes to make it feel like life-or-death to them?
- Write a journal entry from the POV of your main character that addresses what it would be like if they don't win.
- Take time to understand the stakes from all your

characters' points of view. Consider not only what your main character has at risk, but also your antagonist. If they're also well motivated, it will drive the story forward.

Chapter Twelve

Motivation

- What is your character's motivation in the book?
- Does this motivation change?
- How can you make this motivation even more important to them? Are they pushed or pulled or both?

Chapter Thirteen

How to measure conflict in your manuscript

- Consider using the notecard exercise to track conflict levels in your own manuscript.
- Are there ways you can vary the type and intensity of your conflict?

Made in the USA
Middletown, DE
12 September 2020